Alex Telman

Published by Alex Telman, 2025.

While every precaution has been taken in the preparation of this book, the publisher assumes no responsibility for errors or omissions, or for damages resulting from the use of the information contained herein.

THE EPIC OF NOAH

First edition. January 27, 2025.

Copyright © 2025 Alex Telman.

ISBN: 979-8230099994

Written by Alex Telman.

Table of Contents

Author's Note 1
Introduction 2
Part 1: The Call of the Ark 4
Part 2. The Burden of the Flood 11
Part 3: The Burden and the Promise 17
Part 4: The Ark of Faith: Noah's Vision and Duty 23
Part 5: The Building of the Ark 29
Part 6: The Mockery of Noah 36
Part 7: The Ark Takes Shape 42
Part 8: The Final Hours: The Test of Faith 49
Part 9: The Gathering Storm: The Ark and the Beasts 55
Part 10: The Storm's Approach: A Meditation on the Flood 61
Part 11: The Flood Begins 67
Part 12: The Submersion and Hope for Renewal 74
Part 13: Isolation on the Ark 81
Part 14: The Chaos of the Flood 90
Part 15: Moments of Deep Reflection 97
Part 16: Time Passes on the Ark 104
Part 17: Reflection; The Waiting 111
Part 18: The Search for a Sign 118
Part 19: The Waters Begin to Recede 123
Part 20: The Ark Comes to Rest 130
Part 21: The Promise of a New World 139
Part 22: The Renewal of Faith and the Beginning of the New World ... 146
Part 23: Rebuilding Life After the Flood 153
Part 24: The Lingering Questions 161
Part 25: Noah's Final Reflection 169
About Alex Telman 176
Other Titles by Alex Telman 178

Author's Note

The Epic of Noah: In His Own Words is more than a retelling of a familiar biblical story—it is a meditation on faith, obedience, and the depths of human resilience in the face of divine calling. The story of Noah has resonated through generations as a symbol of both judgment and redemption. Yet, beneath the surface of this ancient narrative, I believe there is a deeper, more intimate story to be told: the personal journey of a man who, despite his doubts and the overwhelming odds, chooses to trust in a vision greater than himself.

In crafting this work, I sought to explore what it might have been like for Noah—an ordinary man—to receive an extraordinary command from God. How did he process the enormity of the task ahead? How did he wrestle with his faith, especially when the world around him rejected the very idea of a coming flood? What did it mean for him to shoulder the responsibility of preserving life when everyone else laughed in disbelief? These questions guided me as I endeavored to bring Noah's inner life to the forefront, to show his humanity alongside his divinely appointed mission.

This story is not just about Noah. It is about each of us who faces challenges that seem insurmountable, who wrestle with faith in moments of doubt, and who seek purpose even when the path is unclear. *The Epic of Noah* is a reminder that even in our darkest moments, there is a possibility of hope and renewal, and that faith, when tested, can lead us to places of profound transformation.

I invite you, dear reader, to walk with Noah as he builds not just an ark, but a legacy of faith—a faith that endures beyond the storm and into the promise of new life.

With gratitude

- Alex

Introduction

The Epic of Noah: In His Own Words is a powerful reimagining of one of the most iconic stories in human history—the tale of Noah and the Great Flood—told from the perspective of Noah himself. Through his voice, we are invited to witness the profound journey of faith, obedience, and survival that defined his life and the fate of humanity. This book takes us deep into Noah's thoughts, emotions, and struggles, exploring the transformative moments that shaped him into the patriarch of a new world.

The introduction of the narrative sets the stage for an extraordinary exploration of Noah's character, beginning with the foundational experiences that anchored his unwavering faith in God. Part 1 invites readers into Noah's early life, offering a glimpse of the spiritual relationship that began long before the call to build the ark. The moment when Noah first hears God's command to prepare for the coming flood is one of shock and awe, marking the beginning of his divine journey. This section delves into the roots of Noah's deep faith—one built not on miracles alone, but on an intimate, personal trust in God's will.

As the story unfolds into Part 2, we feel the weight of the divine warning resting heavily upon Noah's shoulders. The enormity of the task ahead—building an ark to preserve life in the face of worldwide destruction—creates a profound inner conflict. The burden of responsibility bears down on Noah, but it is through this struggle that his commitment to God's plan deepens. This section reveals the tension between doubt and trust, illustrating the human side of a man who has been chosen to carry out a monumental mission.

By Part 3, Noah's initial shock begins to give way to a resolute acceptance of the challenge. Here, we see his determination to take up the responsibility placed before him. The reaction of his family and community plays a crucial role in this acceptance—Noah is not only called to lead his own household but to maintain a steadfast conviction amidst widespread ridicule. This section sets the emotional tone for the rest of the story, highlighting the delicate balance Noah must strike between his personal faith, the expectations of his family, and the mockery of a society blind to the impending disaster.

THE EPIC OF NOAH

As the narrative progresses into *Building the Ark*, Noah's journey evolves from an internal battle with divine purpose to the tangible reality of constructing the massive vessel. Part 4 begins with the specifics of the ark's design, a process met with both disbelief and determination. The sheer scale of the task is overwhelming, but Noah's belief in God's command fuels his resolve. Part 5 delves into the physical and emotional strain of gathering the necessary materials, showing the relentless effort required to bring the ark into existence. However, as Noah's work intensifies, the mocking voices of the surrounding people become ever louder, building the isolation he feels. In Part 6, we witness the loneliness that marks Noah's journey, as his faith is increasingly challenged by a world that refuses to acknowledge the flood that looms on the horizon. Yet, through it all, the ark takes shape in Part 7, and with every plank nailed into place, Noah's faith grows stronger, preparing him for the journey ahead.

Through this profound retelling, *The Epic of Noah* seeks to bring new depth to an ancient tale. It is a story not just of survival, but of spiritual awakening, of wrestling with doubt, and of embracing a divine calling with both fear and courage. Each part of this narrative draws readers closer to the essence of Noah's experience—a journey that spans the emotional spectrum and echoes with timeless truths about faith, family, and redemption.

Part 1: The Call of the Ark

In days long past, where hills and rivers wind,
    I walked a humble path with heart aligned.
    A child beneath the stars, so wide and bright,
    I marveled at the dawn, the fall of night.
    The earth, with all its bounty, called to me,
    And whispered secrets hidden in the trees.
    Yet though I knew the beauty of the land,
    I felt a stirring deep, I could not understand.

My father taught me well the ways of light,
    To live with honor, truth, and heart upright.
    He spoke of God, of ways both just and kind,
    And in my soul, such teachings filled my mind.
    I walked the earth with reverence for all,
    With simple faith, no thought too great, too small.
    But as the years did pass and seasons turned,
    I saw the wickedness, how hearts had burned.

For men had turned away from Heaven's light,
    Their hearts grew dark, consumed by endless might.
    And I, though righteous, walked a path alone,
    The cries of others echoing in tone.
    I knew the ways of God, the laws divine,
    Yet in the world, I saw no peace, no sign
    That men would turn, would seek to walk His way,
    For sin had crept into their hearts to stay.

It was one night, beneath the sky's vast dome,

THE EPIC OF NOAH

That something stirred within me—deep, unknown.
The air was still, the stars were bright and clear,
When suddenly, a voice I could not hear
Came soft, then roared, as thunder shakes the skies,
And pierced the quiet night with mighty cries.

"Noah, my servant," came the call, so clear,
    "Rise now, and listen—do not doubt, nor fear.
    The world below is filled with wicked ways,
    And I have watched them squander all their days.
    The time has come, the earth must be renewed,
    The wickedness of men has all but sued.
    But you, my servant, with a heart so pure,
    Shall find the way, through trial, to endure."

I stood there, trembling, heart alive with dread,
    Yet something stirred within, a light ahead.
    The words were sharp, yet filled with love so deep,
    A weightless trust, no need for me to weep.
    For in the voice, though laced with wrath and woe,
    I knew the truth that only Heaven knows.
    A call to justice, mercy intertwined,
    And I, with trembling hands, was called to find
    A path, a way, a purpose true and clear,
    Though all around would tremble, quake in fear.

The world, I knew, was broken, filled with sin,
    But God had found me, called me to begin
    A journey that would lead me through the storm,
    A covenant with Him to keep me warm.
    And in that moment, though my soul did quake,

ALEX TELMAN

I knew the steps I'd take would not forsake
The purpose given, deep within my heart,
A plan unknown, yet never to depart.

He spoke again: "Noah, build the way,
    An ark that will sustain you through the day.
    For rain will fall, the flood will sweep the land,
    But you shall stand, with all that you command.
    Take your family, gather creatures two by two,
    And with your hands, I'll guide you to what's true."

The voice then faded, soft as evening's breeze,
    And left me standing there, upon my knees.
    I knew the task ahead would not be light,
    Yet in my heart, I felt the burning bright
    Of trust, of faith, that He would show the way,
    Though none would see the dawn of that new day.

What did I know of floods, of rains so deep?
    Of waters rising, sweeping land to sleep?
    Yet in my soul, I knew the time was nigh,
    To build the path beneath a troubled sky.
    The world would mock, they'd laugh and scorn my name,
    But in my heart, I felt His holy flame.

And so, I stood, a man both strong and weak,
    Before the call of God, I dared not speak,
    But answered simply, with my soul and might,
    "I will obey, through day, through darkest night."
    No more the life I led, nor simple dream,

THE EPIC OF NOAH

But I was called to walk a greater stream.

I sought no fame, no honor would I seek,
    But in His voice, I found the strength to speak.
    For faith, though tested, never would betray,
    And in His light, I knew I'd find my way.
    The journey would be long, the task immense,
    But through His call, I'd find my recompense.

And so the days, they passed, but all was still,
    The voice of God still echoed in my will.
    The world around, oblivious to me,
    Would soon be swept away beneath the sea.
    And though I did not know what lay ahead,
    I walked with God, and I was truly led.

So I began, with trembling hands and heart,
    To heed the call that none could e'er depart.
    The ark was not yet built, the task unknown,
    But in my soul, I knew I was not lone.
    For in that moment, hearing God's command,
    I found my place, and walked with steady hand.

The world has spun its stories, and I—mere dust in the wind—have watched it all unfold.
    I walk through days that blend together, indistinct, the hum of the earth beneath my feet a constant echo of something larger, something I cannot yet grasp. There is a weight in the air, a heaviness I cannot name. I feel it in my bones, in the tension between the wind and the trees, the way the river runs—too fast, too slow. It is as though the world itself is holding its breath.

ALEX TELMAN

I was born into a life of simple things. My father, a man of gentleness and wisdom, taught me how to walk this earth as though it were a gift. He taught me that faith was the solid ground beneath every step, even when the world seemed indifferent. I believed him. I believed in the stillness of the earth, the clarity of the stars, the soft rhythm of seasons turning. The earth did not ask much of me. It simply asked that I walk with care, with reverence. But I have learned, with time, that the earth does not wait forever for you to listen.

When I was younger, the world seemed open, as if all things were within reach. I thought I understood it—thought I could read it, like a book or a map. But the world, with its heavy pull, has a way of making you doubt your own understanding. And now, in these late hours, when the sun drops below the hills and the shadows stretch long, I wonder if I ever truly knew anything at all.

The people around me—they walk with such urgency, with such deafness. They turn their faces to the sun but do not see it. They see the earth beneath their feet, yet ignore the ground they tread upon. It is as if they are all running toward something they do not understand. And I, I am standing still. I hear them laughing, I see them playing, and it stirs something in me, a quiet anger, a sorrow I cannot explain. They live as though the earth will hold them forever, as though the sun will always rise and the rain will always fall.

They do not hear the world as I hear it. The world that groans beneath the weight of its own history. The world that is tired of its own forgetting.

And then came the voice.

It was not a voice I expected. I was not praying, nor seeking, nor wandering the hills in search of answers. It came in the stillness, in the moments when I was alone with the earth, the air, the weight of time. One evening, as the stars blinked quietly overhead, I heard it—soft at first, a whisper caught between the cracks of the world. And then it grew, until it was undeniable. A call that rang through the air like thunder, yet it did not shake the earth beneath my feet. No, it was a call that shook me.

It was God. I do not doubt this. He spoke my name. He called me, as though I were the last man standing in a world that had forgotten its purpose. And He told me, with a kind of gentle finality, that the earth was broken, that the people had forsaken the path, that the end was coming. There would be a flood. The waters would rise, and the earth would be cleansed. And I—*I*—was to be the one to carry the seed of life forward.

THE EPIC OF NOAH

His words were not full of wrath, but of sorrow. And yet, beneath the sorrow, there was something I had never felt before. There was an assurance, a calm that filled my chest and spread through my limbs. I do not know how to explain it. Perhaps it was faith, though I did not understand it then, and even now, it eludes me. Perhaps it was trust.

I was not afraid. Not at first. How could I be? I had never heard a voice like this before. It was as if the earth itself had spoken to me, as if everything that had come before—the days, the nights, the seasons—had been waiting for this moment. The flood was coming, yes. But something else was coming with it. Something new. And I was to be part of it. The thought filled me, not with fear, but with an overwhelming need to do what was asked of me.

"Build an ark," He told me. "Gather your family, take two of every kind of creature, and save them. For the flood will come, and you must carry them to safety."

How strange the words sounded in my ears. Ark. Flood. Safety.

But what else was there to do but obey? The call was clear, though I could not yet see the shape of the thing I was being asked to create. It was not the ark I feared. No, it was not the ark that terrified me. It was the people. It was the world that I knew. How could they ignore the call that I had heard? How could they continue with their lives as though nothing was coming? The world was blind. The world was deaf. I was not blind. I was not deaf. But what could one man do in the face of such a blindness?

I am only one man. I have no great strength, no power beyond what God has given me. But I have my hands, and I will use them. I will build the ark. I will do what is asked of me, though the world around me laughs. I know they will laugh. I know they will mock me for this. But I will not turn back.

The weight of the task is beginning to settle on me, but it is not a burden I cannot bear. It is a weight, yes, but it is also a purpose, and I am beginning to feel that purpose deep in my bones. I have heard the voice, and it has stirred something in me that I cannot ignore. It has changed me, though I cannot yet explain how. I feel it in the way my hands shake when I think of the ark, in the way my heart beats faster when I think of what is to come. There is something greater than the flood that calls to me. There is something beyond the waters, beyond the end of everything I have known.

And so I will build. I will gather. I will wait. And when the time comes, I will stand with my family, and we will be saved. Not because we are worthy, not because we deserve it. But because we have heard the call, and we have answered it.

I do not know how this will end. I do not know if the world will hear or if they will continue to ignore the signs. But I do know this: God has spoken to me, and I will not be silent. I will build the ark, and I will wait for the flood. I will stand firm in my faith, even when the earth shakes beneath me. I will stand firm, because I know, deep in my heart, that this is the path I must walk.

And so, with trembling hands, I begin.

Part 2. The Burden of the Flood

I. The Voice That Echoed
    A voice within the trembling void did sound,
    A whisper first, then thunderously profound.
    It came from realms where time and space are bent,
    From lips unseen, yet filling all with scent.
    "Behold," it called, "the end, the final day,
    When floodwaters shall sweep the earth away.
    But you, O son of man, shall find the way,
    And on the ark, the righteous shall be laid."
    My heart did tremble, for I knew this truth,
    A weight too heavy for my soul, in youth,
    To understand. The flood—its distant cry—
    Would swallow nations, cities, all would die.

II. The Weight of the Ark
    The task was clear, the flood was surely near,
    Yet in my breast, a pulsing doubt would sear.
    How could I build a ship upon the land,
    When none believed the waters would expand?
    My hands, once steady, now did quake with fear,
    For what was I to build but a veneer?
    A fool's retreat against the ocean's tide,
    A refuge sought but never justified.
    The earth was dry, and laughter filled the air,
    They called me mad, and in their mockery, they dared
    To ask, "Where is your flood? Where is your proof?
    The heavens give no sign, nor tell the truth."

III. The Weight of the Soul
    Yet still I labored, though my heart did cry,

For in my soul, the storm began to rise.
To stand alone, against a mocking throng,
To trust in whispers, where the winds belong—
It was a weight my soul was not prepared
To carry. Who could fathom what I shared?
The skies, though clear, held secrets in their fold,
The earth, so firm, would soon be drenched with gold—
The gold of wrath, the shining grief of death,
The end of all things, the breaking of breath.

IV. The Struggle of Faith
    I prayed, I prayed with trembling hands and knees,
    For guidance, Lord, and clemency from these
    Fears that assailed my thoughts and darkened skies.
    But in my heart, the voice of God did rise:
    "I chose you, Noah, to prepare the way,
    To teach the world, to save the few who stay."
    The words were sharp, like swords within my chest,
    I knew my duty, but could find no rest.
    My mind did whirl in stormy seas of doubt,
    "Will they believe me? Will I find a way out?"
    But God had spoken, and His will was clear,
    A path to walk, though unknown, I must adhere.

V. The Burden of the Ark
    And so I built. Through sun and moon and storm,
    The ark took shape—an ancient, timeless form.
    Each nail I struck, a tear from my heart spilled,
    For I knew not what I made, nor what I willed.
    Yet faith demanded that I take this task,
    Without a question, without a mask.
    Each beam, each plank, each rope, each turning wheel,

Became my soul's companion in its seal.
The ark, the vessel, heavy with my plight,
Would bear the weight of God's own fearful might.
A burden wrought of sorrow, truth, and grace,
It would endure while others met their place.

VI. The Weight of the World
As days turned months, and months then years did flow,
The flood I knew, yet still it did not show.
And in my heart, the longing grew to flee,
To walk away, to save myself and see
The fruit of faith was bitter on my tongue,
A task so great, a weight I'd never hung.
But still I labored—still I took each step,
To build, to craft, to shape what I had kept.
And though the world around me laughed and scorned,
I heard His voice, and in it, I was warned:
The flood shall come; you must not wait nor cease.
I have declared it; you must find your peace.

VII. The Quiet Before the Storm
Now as I stand upon this firm earth's rim,
I know the storm is coming, cold and grim.
The skies are clear, the sun's bright rays do shine,
Yet still I feel the darkness, deep, malign.
The flood is near, though none can see its face—
The storm is calling, it will leave no trace.
But I have heard it; I have known the sound,
The fury that will tear the world aground.
And in my heart, I carry this great weight,
The flood, the promise, and the heavy fate.
The ark, my heart, must carry more than wood,

But souls—both righteous and the misunderstood.

VIII. The Burden of Knowing
    God gave me sight, but sight is heavy, friend.
    To know the end—no hope, no way to bend.
    I walked in peace, yet trembled in my soul,
    For how could one prepare for such a goal?
    The flood is coming, and I cannot delay—
    A task so great, it nearly led me astray.
    But still I stand, though weary, broken, torn—
    For through this weight, a new world will be born.

I don't know why I am still awake. The stars are far too distant, too indifferent to what I've been through. I've been building this ark for so long now that the hammer, the nails, the wood feel like they are part of my body—an extension of some higher power I didn't choose. I am breathing, yes, but I feel my soul pulling further away. I can feel it in the cracks in my bones, in the tension in my jaw, in the silence that keeps seeping in between the blows of the hammer. Each thud is a drumbeat in the long night, and each splinter of wood tears something inside of me that cannot be mended by this task, by any task.

The sky above is too calm for what I am meant to do. The earth is dry, the air is still. Yet the flood, the flood is coming. I hear it in the depths of me, I feel it pushing against the ribs of my chest, pounding on the hollowed chambers of my heart. It is not the sound of water; it is the sound of time, of something slipping from my grasp, something inevitable.

I don't speak of this to anyone. I cannot. I don't think anyone would understand if I did. It's as if I've been given the knowledge of the end of the world, and the weight of it presses down on me like the very floodwaters will. How do you carry something like this? How do you build a monument to what is meant to destroy everything else? They think I'm mad. I can see it in their eyes—the way they laugh and shake their heads. I have heard their words behind my back, their mockery carried in the wind like dust. "The madman, the

THE EPIC OF NOAH

fool," they say, "building his boat for no reason." How can I explain it to them when I do not understand it myself?

They say there is no flood coming, that the earth will remain as it is, and that the heavens will not change their course. How do I explain to them that I know, with every fiber of my being, that it is all true? That the sky, although beautiful, is only a prelude to something darker, something vast? The storm is not of this world, and yet it will become it. How do I tell them that I have heard the voice of God, that He has spoken to me in words that cut through all of time, that pierce the core of my very being? How do I tell them that He has commanded me to build an ark—a refuge—for what? For life, for something greater than all of us, and yet so fragile. For what does God want from me, from us, from this world that doesn't believe?

Some nights, when the hammer falls silent and the wood feels like a weight too heavy for me, I sit by the edge of the campfire and let the stars blink above me, like the indifferent eyes of some celestial judge. It is then that I feel the pressure, the incredible weight of what I must do. It is not the ark itself, nor the flood that presses upon me—it is the knowing. The knowing that the world I was born into, the world I have known my whole life, is slipping away from me, and I am the only one who can see it. No one else sees it. They can't see it. They cannot hear the thunder that vibrates in my chest, the rumble that shakes the bones of the earth.

Sometimes I wonder if I can even bear it myself. How does a man carry such a burden? How does one man hold the fate of creation in his hands and not collapse under it? I wish I could tell someone, but what would they say? They would tell me I am mistaken. They would tell me it is only a storm, that this too shall pass, that it will never come. But I know, I know, it is not a storm. It is the end of everything. And I am standing at the precipice of it, with no one to guide me. Only the voice of God, calling from the dark, calling from a place beyond me, beyond time.

I used to think of faith as something simple. You believe because you trust. You trust because you believe. But it is not that simple. Faith, when it is true, is not easy. It is heavy. It does not come without sacrifice, without pain. It is a constant, grinding weight, the knowledge that you are walking a path no one else can walk with you, that you are carrying something so vast it could crush you if you let it. I've tried to walk this road lightly, but I am learning that there is no light way to carry a world.

Each stroke of the hammer feels like a wound. With each nail, I feel the sting of my own vulnerability. I've built this ark for the future, yes. But it is not the future I am afraid of—it is the silence in the present. The silence that envelops me every time I set down the hammer and let the weight of the task pull at me. The silence that comes when I look around and see no one else. I am alone in this. Alone with the knowledge of the flood, of what is coming. Alone with the voice of God that still echoes in my mind, even now.

And yet, I cannot stop. I will not stop. I can feel the flood, even now, pulling at the edges of my mind. It is as inevitable as time itself. And if I am to bear this burden, to carry the weight of what I must do, then I must build. I must create the ark, for it is the only salvation that remains.

I am a man who has been called to carry the weight of the world, and I must do so. The flood is coming. The ark is my only hope, and I must believe. I must believe that the ark is more than just wood and nails, more than a ship to carry us through the waters. I must believe that it is a symbol of hope—a symbol that there is something greater than this world, greater than the mockery, greater than the fear. There is a divine plan, a purpose to this madness, and I will trust in it.

The world will mock me, and the flood will come. I will not be here to see it. But the ark will carry what is left—life, hope, faith. And I will have done my part. That is all that I can do. It is all that I must do.

Part 3: The Burden and the Promise

I stood upon the threshold of the world,
    The sky above like steel, the earth below a darkened sea.
    A voice had called from the endless void,
    A voice that pierced the stillness like the cry of a child.
    "Build," it said, "Build and bear the weight of all."
    The world, in its silence, did not answer.
    But I, the chosen, the reluctant servant,
    Knew that the command was both my doom and my salvation.

I turned from the wind, turned from the empty night,
    And there, amidst the quiet hum of ancient trees,
    I felt it settle deep within my bones:
    The weight of the promise, the burden of the task.
    God spoke again, His voice like thunder,
    The fire of His will igniting the very air.
    "Make ready," He said, "The storm is near,
    But you shall save, you shall carry life."

I trembled then, for I, too, was only dust—
    A man of clay, of earth, of sweat.
    And yet, within me burned a fire of knowing,
    A calling that reached beyond time, beyond form.
    For how could one man carry the weight of all?
    How could the ark be built by mortal hands alone?

Yet the hand of God reached down, and I understood:
    Faith, like the flood, would carry me.
    With trembling heart, I knelt and took His word,

ALEX TELMAN

And the world became a place where the flood would come,
Yet the ark, the ark would rise.

I gathered my sons—Shem, Ham, and Japheth—
    Their faces like my own, but filled with youth's fire.
    And with them, I began to shape the wood,
    To lay the beams, to set the timbers high.
    The work was slow, the days stretching like the horizon,
    But each strike of hammer to wood
    Was an offering, a sacrifice to the One who called.

I looked into their eyes, my sons, my blood,
    And saw the fire of their own confusion.
    They knew not what I knew, could not see what I saw.
    How could they? How could anyone?
    But in their eyes, I saw the trust—
    The trust of children who know their father
    And follow him into the unknown.

We worked as one, our hands stained with sweat,
    The planks of cedar growing taller with each passing day.
    But still, in my heart, the flood loomed,
    A distant thunder that rattled my bones.
    Would they understand? Would they follow?
    The world outside scoffed, its laughter a bitter wind.
    And yet, in the quiet, I knew my duty.

My wife, Naamah, stood by me—
    Her hands, too, were rough, but her eyes were steady.
    She, too, had heard the voice.

THE EPIC OF NOAH

She, too, felt the call.
And though the burden lay heavy upon my shoulders,
She shared it with me, as wives share the fate of men.
Her silence spoke more than words ever could,
Her love, a balm for the ache that would not cease.

We worked together, the family bound by more than blood,
    Bound by the knowledge that we were the last.
    The last of a people who would see the dawn,
    The last of those who would carry the flame.
    And though the world mocked and scorned,
    I knew we were doing what was right—
    What must be done, no matter the cost.

The ark rose like a monument to faith—
    A testament to the promise, the word,
    That God had given me to carry.
    And in the distance, I saw the storm gathering,
    The winds, the clouds, the darkness coming.
    But I did not fear.
    I did not run.
    I stood firm, my hand in the hand of the One who called.

For though the storm would come,
    The ark would save.
    And I, Noah, would stand as witness
    To the power of faith, the power of the Word.

The voice came like a whisper, soft but powerful. The wind had not spoken before, nor had the earth, and now both seemed to pause, holding their breath for what would follow. There are moments in a man's life when time stops, when it feels as though the world has folded upon itself, waiting for the verdict, and in that moment, I stood. No sound but the pulse of my own blood in my veins, and then that voice again—clear, commanding, reverent: *"Build, Noah. Build the ark."*

And just like that, my life changed. The weight of it, the enormity of the task, landed on me like a stone dropped into water. There was no mistaking it; this was a calling that could not be undone. A task too great for one man, yet here I was, singled out.

But who am I to carry such a burden?

I have always been a man of the earth, a man of simplicity. My hands have known the feel of soil and stone, the rhythm of work, the joy of building something steady, something true. But this—this was different. This was not a house or a well, not a garden to tend. This was a vessel to carry life through the end of the world. How could I, a man of dust, be asked to build something that could carry the essence of creation itself?

I remember the silence in the air that followed the voice. The earth felt like it was holding its breath, waiting for my answer. I don't know what I expected in that moment. A thunderclap? A bolt of lightning? Instead, there was only a profound stillness, as if all creation itself was caught between God's command and my response. The enormity of what I had been asked to do weighed down upon me in that silence. And yet, what was I to do? The command was clear. The weight of it pressed into my chest like a stone I could not move.

I have spent my life laboring under the sun, my hands calloused and worn, knowing the day's work would end and the next would begin. But this work—this work would not end. It would be a task that would span years, that would span lifetimes. It was the kind of work that would define everything.

I stood there in the quiet, the voice of God still ringing in my ears, and yet I felt—what? Fear? Doubt? Yes, those too. But I also felt the stirrings of something else, something I had never known before: a sense of purpose. A purpose so great, so all-consuming, that it drowned out the world around me. I realized, then, that this was not about me. It had never been about me. It was about something far greater. A promise. A salvation. Something that would transcend me and my time on this earth.

THE EPIC OF NOAH

And yet, I still had to ask myself: Could I do this? Could I build this ark? Could I follow this calling to its end, even when I knew it would lead me into the unknown?

I remember turning to my sons. They were there, of course, watching me. My sons—Shem, Ham, and Japheth—who had followed me through every season of our lives. They had worked beside me, had known the quiet rhythm of the land as I did. But this task was unlike any other. They had seen me build homes, carve pathways, plant the earth. But this... this was something else entirely. And I could not tell them. I could not speak the words that hung in the air between us. How could I? How could I explain something so vast, so incomprehensible, to those who had only ever known what their hands could touch, what their feet could stand upon?

And yet, they followed me. I had only to speak, and they would listen. They were my flesh and blood, and their trust in me was as steady as the soil beneath our feet. But even as I saw their willingness, their unquestioning loyalty, I wondered if they, too, felt the same fear that gnawed at my bones. What would it be like, I wondered, to carry a burden not of my choosing, but of God's will?

Then there was Naamah. My wife. I looked at her then, standing silently beside me, her hands calloused from a lifetime of work, her face serene and strong. She had always been the one to ground me, to pull me back when my thoughts began to spiral into chaos. And yet, this time, there was no such solace in her eyes. Her silence spoke volumes. She had heard the call too. She knew what was coming, what had been asked of us. And in her silence, I saw not fear but resolve. She would stand with me, as she always had. She would share this burden.

As we began to prepare, I turned my mind to the task at hand. The ark, I knew, would take years to build. I would need to find the finest wood, to shape it with care, to construct something that would hold through the storm and the fury of the flood. Every nail that went into the timbers was a prayer. Every board, every beam, every plank was an offering to the One who had commanded it.

I look back on those early days now, when the work was new and the burden still fresh. There was no certainty in those moments—only the knowledge that I had been given a task that would outlast me, that would outlast even the generations that came after me. I was not building a house. I was building the future.

And yet, as I worked, I found that there were moments of grace. There were moments when the weight of it all seemed to lift, when the task itself became a kind of prayer, when I could feel the hand of God steadying my own, guiding me forward. I would look at my sons as they worked beside me, their sweat mingling with mine, and I knew that this was not just about saving the creatures of the earth. It was about preserving something greater than ourselves—the essence of life, of creation, of hope itself.

But there were also moments when doubt crept in. The world outside was not kind. It mocked us. It laughed at our efforts, at our faith. They did not understand. They could not. And in those moments, I wondered—what if they were right? What if I had misunderstood? What if the flood would not come, and I had wasted my life on a vision that had no foundation?

But each time doubt rose, I would feel the whisper of that voice again. And it would steady me, calm me. It was a reminder that I was not alone in this, that the burden was not mine to carry alone. God had called me, and with that calling came the strength to endure, to press on, to finish what had been set before me.

I cannot say, even now, if I fully understood what I was doing then. But I know this: I was not merely building a boat. I was building the future. I was carrying with me the essence of all that had been and all that would be. I was carrying hope itself. And with that, I knew that no matter the weight of the task, no matter the mocking of the world or the doubts that rattled my bones, I would press on.

For I had heard the voice of God, and I could not turn away.

Part 4: The Ark of Faith: Noah's Vision and Duty

I. The Call to Construct
    In silence deep, beneath the azure sky,
    A voice again, like thunder, filled the air,
    Yet soft as morning's whispering sigh,
    Told me to build a refuge from despair.
    "Take ye the wood, and build it strong and wide,
    A vessel large enough to stand the tide.
    Make rooms within it, set it firm and tall,
    For the flood shall come, and sweep away them all."
    My hands grew still—what words had I just heard?
    An ark to carry life? To shield and save?
    The weight of it, a burden deep as earth,
    Yet from that task, no mortal could escape.

II. The Beginning of the End
    How could such hands, so weathered and so frail,
    Erect a ship that in its depths could sail?
    I, who had known the toil of mortal soil,
    Now found myself in awe of heaven's toil.
    But as the voice did echo through the trees,
    I felt the stirrings deep within my knees—
    A trembling force, as if the world did bend,
    And all creation knew its coming end.
    "Measure the length, and cut with steady hand,
    Two hundred cubits long, and wide as planned.
    Make it three stories high, with room to spare,
    For every living creature, everywhere."
    And in my heart, the weight of doubt arose,
    How could one man bear such a heavy load?
    What kind of task, what work, was this I'd take?

ALEX TELMAN

Could any mortal bear the flood's great wake?

III. The Blueprint of Eternity
    I paced and stared upon the earth before,
    My mind a whirlwind, thoughts like waves did roar,
    For how could I, so bound by earthly toil,
    Construct a vessel that would never spoil?
    The instructions came like smoke across the sky—
    The light, the words, they shimmered and passed by.
    In deep confusion, I began to trace,
    Each line and angle, in its sacred place.
    "Make it of gopher wood, so firm, so true,
    Pitch it within and without, to hold the blue.
    The window high, and door at side so grand,
    This ark shall be the only saving land."
    The dimensions swam, the air too thin to breathe,
    Could such a ship be made? Could I believe?
    Yet from that moment—still, a spark did rise,
    A trembling faith that lit my weary eyes.

IV. The Weight of Creation
    What marvel this—this task that none had seen,
    A ship to carry life, from every stream,
    From beast to bird, from creeping thing to fish,
    I must protect them all—this sacred wish.
    Noah, what do you see? What do you know?
    The ark will bear the light of life below.
    Each nail and beam a promise to uphold,
    A hope that in this ship, the world turns bold.
    The winds did stir, the waters still remained,
    But I was bound by will, by faith sustained.
    Not even time could shake my steady mind,

THE EPIC OF NOAH

For in my heart, the ark I had to find.
The dimensions set, the wood as I had seen,
I began the work—yet still, the world unseen.
The ark took shape beneath the sky's high dome,
A sacred cradle carved from earthly stone.

V. The Burden of Hope
And as I worked, I thought upon the day—
The flood that would come soon to wash away
The sin of men, the sorrow in their hearts,
The wrath of Heaven in its fearful parts.
I questioned not the call; it rang too true,
Though filled with doubts, I pressed the vision through.
The ark, the flood, the world that would be lost—
I could not turn away, no matter cost.
Each hammer strike, each cut upon the wood,
Seemed to echo cries from souls misunderstood.
For how could they believe in what they could not see?
How could they trust in what was meant to be?
I built the ark with faith—though doubt did gnaw,
Each nail a prayer, each beam a sacred law.
The burden placed upon my weary hands,
A promise, heavy as the shifting sands.

VI. The Final Command
And when the work was near to reach its end,
A final word, a message to extend:
"Bring forth thy family, thy sons, thy wife,
For only they shall pass through to new life.
The beasts of earth, from great to small, to bring,
Two of each—by faith, the animals sing."
And then it dawned upon me in that light—

What had I built? What had I wrought this night?
A refuge born of wood, of faith, of fear,
A vessel for the heavens' promise clear.
The world would drown, but in this ark would rise,
A second chance beneath the ancient skies.
I stood before it, trembling but prepared,
For what would come, and all that I had shared.
The storm would break, the heavens would declare,
And through the ark, I'd know that I was there—
A man of dust, a builder of the sky,
With trembling hands and heart that dared to try.

When I first heard the voice, it came like thunder, low and distant, a tremor in the air. I thought it was my mind betraying me. A whisper wrapped in the sound of a storm, or perhaps it was the wind in the trees. My hands were still—still in the dirt, still in the air, still in a moment that stretched out to eternity—and the voice told me, "Build."

Build what? I wondered, but the answer wasn't far behind. The ark, the vessel to save the earth. Save it from what? A flood, a cleansing so great it would wash away all that was corrupt. And I—why me? What kind of man am I to bear such a burden?

I stood there, my heart pounding in my chest. I wanted to deny it. I wanted to turn around and walk back to the simple life I had known—the life of farming and family. But the voice held me there, pressing me into the earth, as if it had been waiting for me all my life. It was a voice I had known, though I had never heard it before. It was my father's voice, my mother's voice, the voice of the earth itself.

"Build," it commanded again, and this time there was no hesitation in me. No more doubt. The decision had already been made, even before I had understood it. I would build. I had no choice but to build.

I began the first steps, gathering wood, measuring the earth, preparing my hands for the work. The instructions came in fragments, piece by piece, each more detailed than the last. The dimensions—two hundred cubits long, fifty

THE EPIC OF NOAH

cubits wide, thirty cubits high—took root in my mind. And so I began. It seemed impossible at first, the weight of it all. How could one man, even one who walked with God, build something so vast?

I measured the wood, I carved the timbers, I drove the nails through them, and still, the questions persisted. Why? Why this? Why me? What if I fail? What if the flood doesn't come? What if I am mocked and rejected by my people, by my family? I heard their laughter, distant but real, the sneers of those who had no faith, who saw only madness in my eyes.

But every morning, the voice came again. A whisper. A command. The ark must be built.

I looked at my sons, watching them as they worked beside me. They were young, too young for this. They didn't understand the magnitude of what we were doing. I could see it in their faces—the way they glanced at each other, their confusion barely hidden behind their sweat. They worked because I asked it of them, because they were my sons, and what choice did they have? But I could see it in their eyes—they were afraid. And so was I.

How could I protect them from what was coming? How could I promise them safety when I was uncertain myself?

The days stretched on, one after another, like a river I couldn't swim across. The work was endless, but so was the weight of responsibility. I built not for myself but for the earth, for the future. Each nail, each beam, each plank was a testament to my faith and to my fear.

There were moments, in the quiet between the hammering, when doubt slipped in like a shadow, cold and consuming. What if God had chosen wrong? What if the flood wasn't coming? What if I had misunderstood? What if this ark, this enormous structure of wood and sweat, was nothing but a foolish dream? What would the people think when they saw it? They would laugh, they would mock me—and yet, I couldn't stop.

I couldn't stop because I had heard the voice. And the voice had told me to build.

I remember one night, long after my sons had gone to sleep, I sat alone beneath the stars. The ark loomed before me, half-formed and yet already a monument to something greater than myself. The sky was vast and silent, and for a moment, the weight of it all pressed down on me. It was more than just a task. It was the very fate of humanity that lay in my hands. How could one man bear this? How could one man carry the future?

But the voice was there again. Not in the wind or the trees, but deep inside me. The ark will save you, it said. It will save the creatures, and it will save your family. Trust it. Trust me.

And I did.

There were no more questions after that. The doubts remained, but they were no longer mine to answer. The flood would come, and we would be ready. We would be ready because I had heard the voice, and I had trusted it. I had no choice but to trust it.

The ark grew larger as the days passed, and I watched it take shape like the world itself taking shape. Each part of it was a promise, not just to me, but to the earth, to the creatures who would take refuge within it, to the future that would rise from the ashes of the flood. Every nail was a prayer, every beam a hymn. I built not because I understood, but because I believed. And that belief became my strength.

The world outside the ark seemed distant, even as I heard the whispers of mockery from those who passed by. They didn't understand. How could they? They didn't hear the voice. But I did. I heard it, and I could not turn away.

The task was impossible, but the impossible is what faith is made of. The ark was impossible, but I built it.

I remember the first time I looked at the completed vessel, standing there in the fading light, towering above me. It was more than just wood and nails—it was a covenant, a promise, a lifeline. It was everything I had worked for, everything I had hoped for. And in that moment, I knew that whatever the future held, I had done what was asked of me.

I had trusted the voice, and in trusting, I had built a new world.

Part 5: The Building of the Ark

I.
>The dawn of labor broke upon my bones,
>And every step felt harder than the stones
>I moved from earth to sky. The trees were tall—
>Great cedars, thick and strong, yet I must haul
>Them down, from heaven's whispers to the ground,
>Each bark-scarred limb a promise, and each sound
>Of axe upon the trunk a hymn of toil,
>A prayer that sought to pierce the air and spoil
>The peace that had existed here before,
>The world untouched, the earth untouched, once more.

II.
>I took the axe in hand, and with a breath,
>The steel did bite the wood—an echo's death.
>The trees did groan and shudder, bending low,
>As though they knew the task, the final blow.
>My heart did quiver, my hands did shake with dread,
>For what was sacred now lay far ahead.
>The wood, the beams, the ribs, the ribs, the ark—
>A symbol of salvation, cold and stark.
>Each swing of mine that fell, a shadow cast,
>A sign of what was coming, fast, too fast.

III.
>And yet the trees fell silent to the ground,
>Their trunks now lying scattered all around.
>What once was life now lifeless, stripped and bare—
>The forest knew its purpose in despair.
>I could not see the end, but in the deep,

ALEX TELMAN

    The flood was coming, and I could not sleep.
    The sweat upon my brow like streams of salt,
    The weight of what I did, a crushing fault.
    For what would happen to this world once more?
    What would remain when all the flood was o'er?

IV.

    I built the beams, the planks, the walls, the door,
    Each stroke a whisper to the ancient lore.
    And though my body trembled with the strain,
    I felt a strength inside, a steady flame.
    God's words had set me on this holy course—
    To build, to gather, with relentless force.
    But in the quiet hours, alone at night,
    Doubt crept like shadows creeping into light.
    Was I the right one for this sacred task?
    Was there another choice behind God's mask?

V.

    I turned my face to heaven, eyes aglow,
    And asked Him once again if He would show
    The meaning of this burden, this great weight—
    The task He gave to me, this twisted fate.
    And in that moment, as the stars did bleed,
    I felt His voice—a steady, calming reed:
    "Your doubt is not a sin, but part of you,
    For in the dark, My light will guide you through."

VI.

    And so I stood, renewed, my will reborn,
    And worked beneath the sun and with the dawn.

THE EPIC OF NOAH

My hands grew calloused, blistered from the strain,
Yet still I worked, and though the wind would rain,
I carried on. Each nail, each plank, each beam,
A testament to faith—a waking dream.
The ark was rising slowly, brick by brick,
Its bones a fortress strong, its heart so thick.

VII.

The animals would come, I knew, at last,
Each pair, each kind, each future from the past.
And yet, the weight of building shook my mind,
The strain upon my body made me blind
To all but wood, and earth, and nail, and flame—
To everything I'd given to this name.
I felt the hours blur, the days grow long,
The burden pressing deeper, strong, too strong.
Yet even in the storm that tossed my soul,
I knew that this would make the world whole.

VIII.

But then the whispers—doubts began to crawl,
They gnawed at my resolve, they bent my will.
Why must I labor here, and suffer still?
For what end, what cost would this endeavor fill?
I watched my sons, their faces set in stone,
Not yet aware of what would come, alone.
Their hands were steady, sure, their eyes alight,
Yet I alone could see the coming night.

IX.

I wondered if the world would ever see

ALEX TELMAN

The fruits of what this labor would decree.
For all the strain, the blood, the sweat, the pain—
Could all of this withstand the coming rain?
Would men look back and say, "A just man lived,"
And what reward would I, in turn, be given?
For none could know the cost, the weight of truth—
For faith is born in agony and youth.

X.

And so I built, through days of endless work,
Through nights of toil when every sinew jerked.
The animals were near, the pairs were found,
And in their cages, peace did reign profound.
I built the ark, and every beam and nail
Was steeped in grief, but held by love's soft veil.
For through the strain, I knew it had to be—
The flood would cleanse the earth, the world, the sea.

XI.

And when the ark stood proud against the sky,
My soul did swell with tears, but no more cry.
For I had built it—strong and tall, complete—
A vessel of salvation at my feet.
I looked upon the work of hand and mind,
And knew that in the flood, we'd all be kind.
The earth would drown, the heavens would unfold,
But in the ark, our future would be told.

XII.

The wood, the nails, the ark, the earth, the sky—
All were swept away, yet we remained, to fly.

THE EPIC OF NOAH

No man could know the depths of what I felt,
The strain of doing what my heart had dealt.
But in the labor, I had come to see—
That faith is built, one nail at a time, in me.

The air is thick. I feel the weight of it like a stone in my chest. The land around me is quiet, the earth shuddering only occasionally, as though it, too, is aware of what is coming. But for now, the world still seems to breathe, as it always has—slowly, deliberately, with the pulse of ancient rhythms.

Yet the trees—they are coming down. The sound of the axe is a strange one, reverberating against the stillness of the world. The crack of bark, the tearing of wood, all serve as reminders. I had no choice. I had to begin. God had given me the plan: build the ark. I am the one chosen to gather the world into a small wooden vessel. All that is good and pure. All that is worthy.

Each swing of the axe goes deeper, further into the sacred silence that once enveloped the world. It is not just the trees I take down, but the world itself. I watch them fall—tall, majestic trees that were once a part of the landscape, their roots deep in the earth, their branches brushing the heavens. Now they lie before me, sprawled in defeat. I am the one causing this. But there is no other way. There cannot be.

The blade bites into the bark, and it splinters. A drop of sweat stings my eye, but I don't wipe it away. I don't stop. There is no time to stop. The work is endless, the days growing long and the nights colder. The strain pulls at me—at my bones, my muscles. Yet it does not stop. It will not stop. I cannot stop.

I remember, in the stillness of the night, the first moment I heard God's voice. It came with such power, so soft, like thunder rolling beneath the earth's skin, like wind through the leaves, yet piercing. How strange to hear such a thing. A command wrapped in a promise. The flood was coming. All that had been before would end in water, and yet, I—just me—was to save what was good. I, a mere man, who had once been afraid of the shadows that moved in the corners of my home, was to save the world. I had no choice. What was I to do? Refuse? How could I? How could anyone?

I turned to my sons. They did not ask why. They simply worked. They built without question, and in their steady hands, I saw the echo of faith. I never wanted this. I never asked for it. I never dreamed that I would be called to such a thing. And yet, it is my task. God has made it mine. I have been chosen.

I look at my sons, who labor alongside me, their faces set with resolve. They do not falter. They do not question. But I do. I question everything. I question whether I am strong enough, whether my faith is pure enough to carry such a task. This weight—it presses down on me every day. And still, I swing the axe. I cut the trees. I build the ark.

The ark. The word itself is both a blessing and a curse. It is a promise of life, but it is also the seal of death for everything else. The animals will come, two by two, and I will watch them climb aboard, side by side, as the waters rise, as the world I once knew fades away. I will never again see the fields as they were, or hear the laughter of my children in the streets. There will only be the ark. And the flood.

I cannot escape it. The weight of what I have to do is too great. But in each piece of wood, in every nail I drive into the timbers, I feel something inside me shift. The ark is taking shape. The flood is coming. And so, I keep working, as if the hammering will drive away my fear, as if the act of building can somehow make the promise of salvation real. It is the only thing I can do. I do not know how to pray for strength. I know only how to build.

And yet, in the dead of night, when the stars seem too bright and the moon too full, my thoughts grow heavy. My sons are asleep, their bodies curled on the cold earth beside the fire. But I remain awake, the hammer still warm in my hand. The world is changing. I can feel it in the air, in the soil beneath my feet. The land, the earth—nothing will remain the same. I have no way of knowing if the people will ever understand. The flood is coming, yes, but will they ever know what it means to listen? To hear the warning? Perhaps they will mock me until the very end.

The day is long. The sun beats down upon my back, the sweat stinging my skin, the weight of it nearly unbearable. My hands ache, and my bones groan beneath the burden of the work. But still, I build. I cannot stop. I must not stop.

And when I look out at the land, when I see the trees fallen at my feet, when I hear the whistle of the wind through the beams of the ark, I realize—there

THE EPIC OF NOAH

is no going back. There is no turning around. This is my purpose. My task. My calling.

I thought, once, I could turn away. I thought I could run, hide, live in the wilderness where the call would not find me. But I am here. And I will not leave. I will finish what I have started. I will see the ark rise from the earth. I will build it, nail by nail, beam by beam, until it is complete. And when the waters rise, when the flood comes, I will not question. I will not hesitate.

There is nothing left to do but finish the work. And so, I labor, and the land trembles beneath my feet, and the sound of the hammer is the sound of a world collapsing. But it is also the sound of something being born. The ark. The flood. The world to come.

And in my heart, I know it is the only thing I can do. I must finish. There is no other way.

Part 6: The Mockery of Noah

The sky was bright, the day unbroken, clear,
    The earth still warm beneath my feet and fear.
    But in their eyes, the questions grew like weeds—
    A whisper spreading through the growing seeds.
    "Is he mad?" they asked. "Is he cursed or lost?
    What burden drives him? What was the cost?"

They saw the ark—this monument of wood—
    And laughed with voices full of bitter blood.
    The hammer's beat, the nails, the work, the wood—
    They mocked it all, for none of them understood.
    "Is he a fool?" they jeered from high and low,
    "Who dares to speak of floods where none can go?"

I walked alone, my sons beside me still,
    They worked in silence, doing God's command.
    Yet all the while, the mocking tongues would spill,
    Their venom tainting all the sunlit land.
    "Where is this flood?" they cried with bitter glee,
    "Why build an ark for what the earth shall not see?"

I turned my face away, but could not hide
    The burning ache that swelled beneath my skin.
    They laughed and danced, their folly deep and wide,
    While I, with every nail, felt sorrow spin.
    Each word of mockery, each cruel refrain,
    A weight upon my heart, a growing chain.

THE EPIC OF NOAH

I could not speak, for what was there to say?
    The storm was far and yet it called to me.
    I built in silence, though the mocking play
    Did tear at what was left of sanity.
    I heard them call me mad, and all the while
    I labored on, alone, without a smile.

"Behold, the fool," they shouted as they passed,
    "His madness grows with every passing day."
    But I, beneath their gaze, must ever last,
    A silent witness to their cruel display.
    Yet in their eyes, no truth did I behold,
    Only the blindness of a world grown cold.

And still the ark arose, each beam a plea,
    A silent prayer against the rising tide.
    I built alone, my family close to me,
    But far beyond, the world was pushed aside.
    I could not silence all their mocking cries,
    For still they mocked, beneath indifferent skies.

Oh, how the world had fallen, how they swore,
    That nothing would come, and all was well.
    Their laughter rang like thunder on the shore,
    Each mock a bell, each jest a poisoned spell.
    I saw their faces twisted in the light,
    Their joy was born from ignorance and spite.

And still I toiled, though isolation grew,
    Though the mocking sun burned higher still.

ALEX TELMAN

My soul, once firm, began to question too,
As doubts crept in, unbidden, unfulfilled.
But deep inside, the spark of faith remained,
And though alone, I would not be constrained.

The earth was vibrant, glowing with its peace,
    The rivers ran, the birds flew through the air.
    But to me, all was bleak, the world's release
    Felt far from me, yet ever present there.
    The people danced, the sky stretched wide and blue,
    While I, in silence, faced a task to do.

"How long, O Lord, must I endure this strain?
    How long must I build for a dream so far?"
    But His voice, though soft, came in the rain—
    "You build, for I shall see you from afar."
    And so I built, though mockery did ring,
    For in my heart, His promise was the thing.

The days stretched out, the years went by, and still
    The world would laugh, and still I heard their cries.
    But in my heart, a quiet voice did fill,
    A still, soft whisper—stronger than their lies.
    "Build, O Noah, for I am close at hand.
    And when the flood comes, you will understand."

The mocking grew, the doubts pressed harder still,
    But in the silence, I held firm, my soul.
    I built, I worked, I honored Heaven's will—
    The ark, my testament, my heart, my goal.

THE EPIC OF NOAH

And when the flood came, swift as morning's rise,
The world would know the truth behind their lies.

They laughed at me, with joy in their cruel eyes,
    And yet they did not know the coming prize.
    The waters rose, the skies began to bleed,
    And all the earth would bow before their need.
    The ark, my only solace in the storm,
    Would be the vessel where the world reborn.

The mockery, the laughter, all would cease—
    For in the flood, there would be no release.
    And I, though mocked, though lost, would stand apart,
    A witness to the end and to the start.
    For in the ark, where all things would take flight,
    There would be hope, a soul reborn in light.

The sun hangs in the sky, high and unforgiving, and I am alone with my work. It has been years now, the years of their laughter, their mockery. I remember the first time I heard it—the sound of their ridicule. It wasn't loud at first, just whispers, murmurs that hung in the air, soft as the first breeze of morning, and I tried to ignore them. But with each passing day, it grew louder. Now it echoes around me, a constant clamor that gnaws at my bones, at my faith.

    They think me mad. They think me cursed. Sometimes I wonder if I've become something more than I was—a shadow of the man I once was, stripped of joy, stripped of hope. They see the ark, this massive structure I've built from wood and sweat, and they do not understand. How could they? No one has heard the voice of God the way I have. No one has felt that weight, the weight of the heavens pressing down on you, telling you that you must do something no one else has ever dreamed of doing. Something that no one else will ever believe.

ALEX TELMAN

I feel their eyes on me. They are not kind eyes. They are full of suspicion, of doubt, of scorn. I can hear their voices as they pass by, their words like stones thrown in the air, meant to land somewhere near my heart. "What is he doing?" they ask, as though they've never seen a man labor for his life's purpose before. "Why is he building this monstrosity? There is no rain. There is no flood. Does he think we will believe this foolishness?" They say it loud enough for me to hear. They want me to hear it. They want to break me. They want me to doubt the very thing that has kept me grounded in this world, that has kept me working when I felt every muscle in my body scream for rest.

I cannot rest. I will not rest.

But in the quiet moments, when the hammer falls silent and the wood lays still, I do not know if I can keep going. The laughter haunts me. It is relentless. It follows me from morning to night, from sunrise to sunset. They mock me with their songs, their jokes. They do not see what I see. They do not hear what I hear. The world is blind, deaf, and stupid, and I am the only one who knows what's coming. What is coming is death. And I am the one who is being asked to save it.

God told me to build the ark. He told me to save the world. I didn't ask for this. I didn't ask for this burden. I was content with my life—simple, quiet. I walked the earth with my sons, with my family, as every man does. But now I am building an ark, and I can feel the weight of it in every breath I take. The ark is not just wood and nails. It is hope. It is salvation. It is the future of all creation, and it rests upon my shoulders alone. Alone. Not even my sons truly understand. They help me, yes, but they do not feel it the way I feel it. They do not know the responsibility that presses down like a mountain, the weight of knowing that if I fail, all is lost.

The people laugh because they do not know. They do not know what I know. They do not know the terrible, beautiful truth that has been whispered to me in the silence. They will not know until it is too late.

Sometimes I think they are right. I wonder if I am truly mad. I wonder if the voice I heard was just the wind, or the fire, or my own mind playing tricks on me. What if I am only building my own tomb? What if the flood does not come? What if I am wrong, and everything I have worked for is for nothing?

But then I think of the ark. I think of the wood, of the nails, of the days and nights spent shaping something that will carry life through the storm. I think

THE EPIC OF NOAH

of the animals, of the creatures who will find refuge in the shelter I have built. And I cannot stop. I will not stop.

The laughter still rings in my ears, louder now, as the people gather in their groups and watch me work. It is a strange thing, to be the object of their disdain. I have always been one of them, a man of the earth. But now I am set apart. I walk in their world, and yet I do not belong to it anymore. I feel as though I am walking through a dream, and I wonder if I will ever wake up from it.

I know what they say about me. They say I am foolish. They say I am mad. But they do not see what I see. They do not feel what I feel. They do not know the fear that grips me every night, the fear that I will fail. They do not know the longing in my heart for the storm to come, for the flood to wash away the world I have known, to cleanse it and make it new again.

And so I build. I build because I have no choice. I build because God has commanded me, and because there is no other path. I build because I am the last hope for this dying world. And though the laughter grows louder, though the doubt gnaws at my heart, I will not stop. I cannot stop. The ark must be built. And when the flood comes, I will be ready.

I think of my family, of my sons. They are with me, working beside me, though they do not fully understand the weight of it all. I see them, their faces set in determination, and I wonder if they feel the same ache in their hearts that I do. I wonder if they hear the same whisper in the wind that tells them this is all for something greater than they can see. I hope they do. I hope that when the flood comes, they will understand. But for now, I must build alone, for I am the one who has heard the call. I am the one who must answer.

And so I hammer. And so I saw. And so I labor. Alone.

But the ark rises, and with each plank, with each beam, I am closer to the truth. The flood will come. And when it does, I will be ready.

Part 7: The Ark Takes Shape

I. The Call of the Wood
    The days stretched long, the wind it howled,
    And in the endless sun, I stood unbowed.
    From soil, from sky, from stone and flame,
    I wrought the will of God in wood and name.
    Each beam a prayer, each nail a vow,
    To shape a vessel for the storm that prowls.
    The trees, once standing tall with crowns of green,
    Now bent beneath my hands, their branches lean.
    I whispered to them, to each timber new,
    And felt their silent strength, their sacred hue.
    The ark takes shape, the walls rise wide,
    A testament to faith, where doubts once tried.
    For what is wood to hands that serve the divine?
    What is strength, but the faith that makes it shine?
    A tremor in my soul, a certainty,
    The flood is coming—this is God's decree.

II. The Weight of the Ark
    The walls grow high, the planks are joined,
    Each curve, each line, a spirit reined.
    The frame of wood, a breath within the air,
    I shape with trembling hands the ark of care.
    Yet every nail that meets the timber's grain,
    I feel it deeper, in my heart, the strain.
    How could I know if this will hold or break?
    How could I know the waters that will wake?
    My faith is tested, every moment passed,
    For with each stroke, I tremble, yet I ask—
    "Is this enough? Will the ark stand firm,
    Or will it falter when the winds confirm?"

THE EPIC OF NOAH

III. The Solid Silence
    And in the silence, when the hammer falls,
    A deeper truth, unspoken, softly calls.
    The ark rises up like mountains from the sea,
    Its bones and sinews stretching wild and free.
    Each board, each cut, a sacred act of grace,
    God's will, transformed in wood, now takes its place.
    I see the shape before me, vast and true,
    As though the ark had risen from the blue.
    And in its form, I sense the presence near—
    A whisper, soft as shadows, yet severe.
    And though I shake, I see His face in light,
    My heart grows sure, my soul alight with might.

IV. The Hope That Grows
    The work is endless, still the days roll on,
    The task not finished, yet my hope is drawn.
    For in this ark, I find my heart reborn—
    Not just the flood, but life beyond the dawn.
    Each plank, each timber, becomes my song,
    A hymn of hope to which I now belong.
    I see the animals that wait, unseen,
    In the soft murmurs of the coming scene.
    The flood will come, yet in the ark I build,
    I find the life that God has long fulfilled.
    His hands within me, shaping wood, shaping time,
    I rise above the fears that once would climb.

V. The Storm Within
    The clouds still gather, heavy, dark, and vast,
    Yet in my heart, a peace that will outlast.

ALEX TELMAN

The ark, once hollow, now begins to hum,
A song of life—its pulse, its beat, its drum.
And though the world, outside, may not believe,
I know the storm will come, and I'll receive
The promise that God gave to me that day,
When He spoke in thunder, soft as clay.
The ark grows higher with each dawn and dusk,
And in my heart, a vision clear, robust:
The flood will come, and I will rise with grace,
For this is not just wood, it's God's embrace.

VI. The Strength of Faith

I've hammered long, my hands are bruised and torn,
Yet still I build, though worn and battleworn.
For every splinter that tears at my skin,
I know the pain is where the truth begins.
With every drop of blood, with every tear,
I lay the ark, I lay my heart so near.
And in its shadow, faith begins to grow,
The deeper truth in every strike I know.
For faith is built not in the calm of light,
But in the fire, in shadows, in the night.
And as the ark takes shape, I take my stand,
A servant of the Lord, by His own hand.

VII. The Assurance in the Wood

Now rise, O ark, in your sacred might,
Your beams are bound, your sails are set for flight.
And though the flood may come with thundered rage,
I know the end is written on your page.
Each plank, each joint, a testament of trust,
A promise held in wood, unbroken, just.

THE EPIC OF NOAH

I see His hands within each nail, each plank,
I feel His presence in the river's bank.
The world may mock, the world may sneer and laugh,
But I will build His vision on my path.
The ark takes shape, the faith within me grows,
For in this work, God's promise brightly glows.
The burden shifts within me, quiet, slow,
For as the ark grows strong, so does my soul.
In wood and stone, in sweat and tears I find,
A deeper peace, a steadfast peace of mind.
The storm may rise, the waters soon may roar,
But I have built the ark, and built it more.

VIII. The Test of Time

With each new dawn, the ark grows ever tall,
A vessel strong enough to face it all.
Its timbers hum with power, pure and wide,
A force that will not break, nor bend, nor slide.
The world may mock, the world may tear apart,
But I will build the ark with faithful heart.
And when the flood comes rushing from the sky,
I will not fear, for I will stand, not cry.
I built the ark, and built it strong and sure,
A shelter from the storm, a hope secure.
No longer lost, no longer torn in doubt,
In this great ark, I know my faith's about.
For every stroke, for every aching bone,
I know the ark will carry me alone.
And when the flood begins, I will stand proud,
For in this vessel, I have found the cloud.

The ark grows, bit by bit, and I feel the weight of it like an anchor tied to my chest. It is as though the timbers are growing with me, as if my own heart beats with the pulse of each hammer blow. Every plank, every nail, every stroke—each one is a prayer, yet it never seems enough. The day slips into night, the moon slides from one side of the sky to the other, but the task never ends. The weight of it all has become so heavy I feel I am submerged in the wood, in the ocean of my work.

At times, I forget why I'm doing this, why the endless labor, why the silence of these long hours that stretch into years. My family—the ones I love—work beside me, their bodies sore, their minds tired. Yet there is no room for complaint, for there is no question. God spoke, and I obeyed. But obedience doesn't mean understanding. How can I explain to them the gravity of what's coming? How can I explain to myself that this is what I was made for, that this wood, this ark, is the salvation not just of my family but of every living thing that draws breath on this earth? The answer comes to me like the thunder I once heard in my soul. A voice inside me that feels both terrifying and warm.

Still, I wonder. Why me? Why us? The earth has turned in its cycle since the first dawn, yet I am the one who carries the burden of the flood. When I sleep, it's as if the waves are already crashing around me. I dream of deep waters, of drowning, of holding my breath so long that I forget what air feels like. But then I wake and the dream is gone, and all I have is the rhythm of my hammer, the song of the nails driving into place.

I think of the others—the people who pass by, who shake their heads, who laugh. They do not understand, they cannot. I see their faces when they look at the ark. It stands, an impossibility, a thing too large for this world. And yet, I cannot stop. How can I? What else is there to do when the voice of the divine calls, when the earth is preparing itself for a cleansing fire? These men and women—they laugh, they mock, they don't see the flood that is coming.

I wish I could explain, but the words catch in my throat, heavy as the beams I carry. What is it that compels me to continue when every part of me longs to break? They say nothing, the crowds that come to watch. Their gazes fall like stones upon my shoulders, but I do not let them break me. I have to believe in this work. I have to believe that it's real, that it matters, that the flood is not a metaphor but something more, something beyond me, beyond us. Perhaps, they say, it's madness. Perhaps, they say, I am the one who's lost his mind. But

THE EPIC OF NOAH

their voices, distant as they are, cannot pierce the truth that I feel deep within me, that pulls me every day to lay down the next beam.

The ark, at first, was a shadow. A dream, a thing that could not be touched. Now, it is solid, real, the weight of it pushing down on the earth. It is not just wood, but the promise of salvation. I feel it in my bones, this vision that has taken shape. The ark is more than a shelter, it is the breath of life.

Still, I struggle. The timbers are heavy. The weight of the world seems to rest on my hands as I lift them to work. My body aches. I feel the sweat on my skin, the strain in my muscles. Sometimes, when I wake at dawn, I want to leave it all behind. The exhaustion threatens to overwhelm me. The thoughts that tell me to quit, to walk away, are always close, whispering in the dark. But I push them back. I must continue. I must believe. There is no other choice.

And then, there are the quiet moments—when the hammer falls and the world falls silent. The only sound is the steady rhythm of work, the steady beat of creation. These moments are like prayers. They fill the spaces between my breaths, between the beats of my heart. They remind me why I do this, why I continue. It's not just for myself, not just for my family. It's for something more. It's for life. For the creatures that will step aboard and the hope that I will carry in the silence of the ark.

Sometimes, I think of the animals. They are an afterthought to some, but not to me. I wonder how they will find their way. How will they know when to come? Will they understand? Will they see what is coming, or will they, too, be lost to the flood? I try not to dwell on such thoughts, but they creep in. Perhaps it is the weight of knowing that every creature, every living thing, depends on the ark for their salvation. Every life that will be spared will owe its survival to this vessel, to this task that I have undertaken.

I speak little to my family. There is no need for words, not anymore. They know what must be done, they understand without question. I watch them, as they work alongside me, and I see the weariness in their eyes. I see the doubt, too, though they try to hide it. There are no assurances, no promises. Only the steady motion of our hands, the rhythm of the work.

I sometimes wonder if they, too, question. If they, too, feel the weight of the task and wonder if it will all be enough. I wonder if they, too, lie awake at night, feeling the weight of the world pressing in on them, pressing down on their hearts. I do not ask. There is no time for questioning. There is only the ark. There is only the work.

As the days pass, the shape of the ark grows clearer. The hull is solid now. The walls rise with strength, with purpose. And I feel the promise in every joint, in every plank. The flood may come. The storm may rage. But I will not falter. The ark is my faith. It is my strength. And I will see it to the end. I have no choice.

The work continues. The world outside laughs, but the ark stands strong. Every day, I build, and every day, I believe.

Part 8: The Final Hours: The Test of Faith

I. The Stillness Before the Storm
    The day has come, and yet it seems so still,
    A moment caught in time, a fragile lull.
    The ark now stands, its wooden bones complete,
    A giant vessel, humbly set to meet
    The coming storm that no one yet believes,
    A flood foretold that none but I receive.
    The air is heavy, thick with fear and doubt,
    And yet within, I hear a silent shout:
    "Prepare, O soul, for all that you have known,
    For all that waits is but the seed to grow."

II. The Call to Enter
    I stand upon the ark's great wooden door,
    And feel the weight of Heaven's final roar.
    A call so ancient, deep as ocean's night,
    Whispers in my ears, a growing light:
    "Enter, O servant, enter and be saved,
    For you have walked the path the righteous paved."
    I turn my gaze towards the rising sky,
    A field of clouds, a mighty army high.
    The heavens open—lightning cracks the air,
    A voice from deep within the thunder's glare:
    "The time has come, and all must now retreat
    Inside this ark, where salvation's fleet."

III. The Sacrifices Made
    I watch the creatures, two by two, advance,
    Their steps so sure, their motions filled with trance.
    A lion's gaze, a dove, a serpent's slither,

ALEX TELMAN

All moving as if summoned by a tether.
I offer them my hands, my steady mind,
And guide them in, though peace I cannot find.
The promise stands, and yet I feel the test—
My faith is frayed, my heart, uncomfortably pressed.
For though the rain has not yet touched the ground,
I sense the weight of what I must unbound.

IV. The Closing Door
    The door is closing, and my soul does quake,
    A final choice that none could ever fake.
    I step inside, the timbers loud with sound,
    A thunderous echo, deep and heaven-bound.
    And yet, as I descend within the ark,
    A trembling light, a shadow cold and stark,
    Begins to creep within my mind and soul—
    I wonder, still, if I am truly whole.
    The weight of years, the weight of fate, does press,
    For even faith must taste its own distress.

V. The First Drop
    Then came the first—a tiny, trembling drop,
    A flicker falling from the heavens' top.
    It strikes the earth, then softens with the rain,
    A warning whispered on the wind's refrain.
    The clouds are thick, and lightning rends the sky,
    Yet still I stand beneath it, wondering why.
    The flood is coming—there can be no doubt,
    But will it come to drown, or lift us out?
    I breathe in deep and close my eyes to pray,
    And hope that faith will guide me through the fray.

THE EPIC OF NOAH

VI. The Test of Faith
    Is this the test, O Lord, that you have set?
    To stand alone, amidst the rising threat,
    To trust, to wait, to know what's yet unseen?
    The ark is full, and all feels yet serene,
    But doubt does curl and creep inside my chest,
    A constant companion, never at rest.
    My mind begins to whisper in the dark:
    "What if this ark will fail, a hollow mark?
    What if this flood is not as true as told,
    What if the storm devours what we hold?"

VII. The Deepest Night
    The rain begins, a drumbeat on the roof,
    And all around us trembles, dark and aloof.
    The floodgates open, and the world starts to drown,
    The land, the beasts, the sky, the ancient town.
    Yet here we sit, in silence, held within,
    And still, the doubt curls deep beneath my skin.
    I think of them—those who mocked, those who scoffed,
    And I wonder if the flood will be enough.
    Will they see us now, safe upon this ark?
    Or will the waters leave us in the dark?

VIII. The Promise of the Dove
    As darkness falls, I turn to all I've done,
    To see this through, to trust what's just begun.
    For though the storm may rage, the winds may roar,
    The voice within is steady at the core.
    And in my heart, a vision stirs and hums—
    The promise of the dove that soon will come.
    The faith I planted deep within my soul,

Now grows and blossoms—an eternal goal.
The flood will pass, the earth will rise anew,
And we, the chosen, will be born from true.

IX. The Storm Unleashed
   The storm unravels, wild and fierce and free,
   Its might unfolding like a history.
   And in the sky, the thunder beats and breaks,
   The earth begins to shudder, bend, and quake.
   Yet still, I stand within this sacred space,
   The ark, a vessel full of heaven's grace.
   I hold my breath, I wait, I wait to see—
   The flood may come, but will it come for me?

X. The Trial of the Ark
   The waters rise, they climb with deadly aim,
   And every corner whispers, "End this game."
   But deep within, my soul has found its place,
   A knowing still, a steady pulse of grace.
   The ark will hold, it will not fall to dust,
   The flood shall pass, and in its wake, I trust.
   The final hour may bring its fearful hour,
   But in this ark, I know my God's great power.

I stand now before the great door of the ark, but my mind is elsewhere—elsewhere, even though the storm is almost upon us. I hear the winds rising, soft but insistent, as if the earth itself is trembling under the weight of what is to come. But my heart, my heart, is too heavy to hear the winds. The winds are irrelevant now. I've heard them before.

God said it would come. And yet, this final hour feels more like a dream than reality. I should feel more sure, shouldn't I? But the quietness of this

THE EPIC OF NOAH

hour, the kind of silence that comes just before catastrophe, feels like a great void—like I'm standing on the edge of something vast and unknowable. It's not that I doubt God's word. No, I've never doubted that. What I doubt now is whether I am truly ready. Ready to fulfill this—this great, crushing weight. I was chosen. But chosen for what? To watch the end unfold?

I hear the creatures stir inside the ark, their movements now a steady rhythm, but their steps cannot drown the turmoil that roils within me. I should be at peace. I've heard His voice, and I've obeyed. But I cannot quiet this incessant voice inside me that questions whether I've done enough. Can anything ever be enough when you are tasked with saving all of creation? The enormity of it is—well, it is almost too much. Too much for a man, too much for one soul to carry. And yet here I am, carrying it.

I look at the wood, the strong timbers that I helped gather, that I shaped with my own hands, and I think of all the hands that never touched this ark. The hands of those who mocked me, who cursed me, who laughed as I built this ship alone. I still hear their voices in my mind, thick with scorn. "What are you building, Noah? What foolishness are you preparing for?" And I answered them with silence. What else could I do? How could I explain to them what I didn't fully understand myself? That there would be a reckoning, a reckoning beyond all earthly understanding, and that I had been chosen to endure it? No one could have understood that. Not even I could understand it. And now, as I stand before the door, waiting for the rain to fall, I realize that nothing, nothing will ever make me understand it fully.

The animals are inside, a living testament to the prophecy. There's something almost sacred in their quietness—no fighting, no fear. They've come. They've entered. The ark is ready. But I feel unready. I feel the weight of something looming—something outside this ship, something that wants to tear through it, to swallow us whole. I wonder how the flood will feel. Will it feel like a cleansing? Or will it feel like the end of everything, even of me? I never asked for this. I never asked to be the last one standing. But here I am.

I think of my family. They have come, too. They've entered this ark with me, and they've trusted me—trusted that I could keep them safe. I see their faces now, in the darkness of the ark, and I hear the quiet prayers that rise from them. We are all praying. Praying for mercy. Praying for deliverance. We have no choice but to trust. But even faith is a trembling thing in the face of what is coming. And so I hold my children close, their hands in mine, as though we can hold on to something real, something solid before the storm breaks.

I think of my wife, her steady presence beside me through all of this. She never wavered, not once. I wonder if she is afraid now, as afraid as I am. But I do not ask her. We have never spoken of our fears aloud—not since the day God's voice first came to me. She must feel the weight of this burden too. I know she does. We all do. But we have been bound together by something deeper than fear now. We are bound by the promise of salvation. We are bound by God's word. And yet, still, still I wonder—will it be enough?

The first drops of rain begin to fall, soft at first, like tears from the sky. I do not look up to see them. I know they are there. I know the storm is beginning. The rain is not a mere sprinkle; it is a warning. A sign that the end of time has arrived. I feel my heart quicken as the sound of the raindrops becomes louder, faster, as though the earth itself is being pressed to its end.

But I do not allow myself to turn back. There is no turning back now. The ark, the animals, my family—these are the only things that matter now. I think of those outside, the ones who mocked, the ones who ridiculed my every step. I think of them now as the water begins to rise, and I wonder if they understand what is happening. But no—there's no time for wondering. It is too late for them. It is too late for anyone who has not believed, for anyone who has not listened. The flood is here, and it will not be stopped.

I close my eyes and breathe in deep, the air thick with the scent of rain, the earth, and the strange, heavy smell of wood and the animals that surround me. We are all breathing the same air now. We are all waiting. I think of the earth outside, the dry land that will soon be swallowed up, and I know this: I do not fear death. I fear not fulfilling the will of God. I fear that this journey—this calling—will be the end of us all.

The rain is falling harder now, and the wind picks up, howling around the ark. I hear the creak of the timbers as they begin to buckle beneath the weight of the storm, but still I stand, and still I wait. I wait for the flood to come and wash away the past. And when it does, when it finally does, I will have no choice but to believe that this was meant to be.

I will have no choice but to let go. And in that letting go, perhaps I will finally understand.

Part 9: The Gathering Storm: The Ark and the Beasts

The world, once silent, hums with fear,
    For the creatures, beasts of earth and air,
    Now tread upon the soil of doom.
    Through shadowed paths, beneath the loom
    Of darkened skies, they come—each kind,
    The wild, the meek, with eyes so blind
    To fate—yet still, they come to me.
    A thrumming pulse, a distant plea.

The lion's roar, the eagle's cry,
    The lamb's soft bleat, the hawk's sharp eye,
    The serpent's hiss, the jaguar's leap—
    They come to enter and to sleep
    Within the walls I've built in trust.
    They come—against the fire of dust,
    Against the clouds that crack and quake,
    As waters rise, and heavens break.

I stand, unmoved, before the door,
    And see them gather on the floor,
    Each pair in awe, and yet aware,
    Of something darker in the air.
    Their paws are soft, their breath is sweet—
    They come to find the end, the seat
    Of judgment in the twilight's glow,
    Before the great deluge shall flow.

ALEX TELMAN

How many, Lord? How many more?
    I cannot count the beasts that pour—
    From hills and valleys, fields and streams,
    They come to me, their steps like dreams.
    The great whales swim in silent grace,
    The stags all race through open space,
    The elephants, with trunks held high,
    All march beneath the darkened sky.

The ark is filled; the chambers swell.
    The creatures call, as though to tell
    The stories of their lives before,
    And still I stand outside the door,
    Wondering, questioning, still unsure—
    For though the ark is sealed in place,
    I know not if I have the grace
    To see this through, to hold the weight—
    The weight of fate, the weight of hate.

I hear the thunder—low and deep,
    It stirs the oceans, wakes the sleep
    Of mountains high, of lands below,
    As if the world has learned to grow
    In pain—its heart now beats with dread—
    The time has come; the flood is spread.
    But still the creatures come and go,
    And in their steps, I feel the flow
    Of God's great will, of His command,
    To cleanse the earth with sea and sand.

I think of all that's left behind—

THE EPIC OF NOAH

The fields, the homes, the love once kind,
The voices that once laughed and sang,
Now gone, their echoes faintly rang.
The world will change; the flood will sweep
And every living thing shall weep—
And yet, amid this grief, I know
That God's hand will not let go.

Each creature enters, one by one,
    The mighty and the small begun—
To fill the ark, to stand in line,
And wait for waters, cold and fine.
A deer, a wolf, a dove in flight—
They pass me by in silent night,
And though I understand their way,
My heart is torn, it cannot stay
The ache of knowing what is near—
The flood, the rain, the trembling fear.

I hear the howling winds grow loud,
    And see the storm's encroaching shroud—
The clouds, the darkening skies above,
No longer a sign of peace, of love,
But judgment drawn in lines of death—
Yet still I wait, with baited breath,
To see the end of all I know,
To see the heavens bend and flow.

I close the door upon their call,
    I see them standing, one and all,
Inside the ark, as heaven roars,

ALEX TELMAN

A thousand storms on distant shores.
The final breath of earth is held—
In sacred silence, all is felled,
The creatures rest, the world is still—
And in this quiet, I feel the chill
Of knowing that the flood is here,
And I—alone—must face the fear.

Oh, Lord—what have I done? What now?
    This ark, this ship, my heart—I bow,
    For in this moment, I am small,
    A man, a servant to Your call.
    And yet, I know that in this place,
    The weight of life and death must face.
    And though the flood may rise in force,
    I place my trust in Your great course.

The ark is full; the creatures sleep—
    The promise made—our souls to keep.
    The storm is here, the rain begins—
    The ark, it stands against the sins.
    And in the darkness, I hold tight
    To God's great mercy, His great might.

I stand before the door, the threshold now sealed, a heavy silence pressing down upon me. The creatures are inside—every one of them, from the towering giraffes to the crawling ants. They've found their place in the darkened hold of the ark, their sounds muffled now, their breathing a chorus of strange harmony. They've come from the earth, the mountains, the valleys, as if driven by something far more powerful than instinct, drawn into this great vessel I have built with my hands, with my faith, and with my fear.

THE EPIC OF NOAH

My hands tremble, though they are still. I can hear the weight of the world behind me, pressing in with a force that feels too immense to be borne by a man like me. I wonder—how many more are out there, in the wild spaces, the places I cannot see? What of those I couldn't reach? What of the voices I couldn't quiet, the faces I couldn't save? I did what I could. I followed the call, listened when the thunder first cracked in my ears, a voice so soft, so sharp. I followed, and I built. I worked as though the very earth had breathed new life into me, as if the beams and planks were some divine expression of my will.

But now, with the door closed, with the ark heavy with life, I feel more uncertain than ever.

The sky is dark. A clouded abyss presses above, and I know—the time is here. The flood is not far now. The storm is coming. It's already upon us in spirit, in the howling winds that beat against the hull of the ark, in the way the earth itself seems to recoil. It is a tension unlike any I have known. The flood will cleanse. The flood will ravage. And I will watch it unfold. I will watch as the waters sweep across the land, erasing everything I knew.

But for now, there is silence. For now, there is only the sound of my breath and the thrum of the ark, the steady pulse of life within it. The animals rest, though they are not still. They are filled with their own unease, their own strange knowing. They, too, sense the world changing. And I—how can I make sense of it? How can I reconcile the promise I have been given, the promise I believed in when I first heard God's call, with the weight I now carry in my chest? The weight of knowing that the world will be wiped clean, that everything will be lost.

I do not know how to prepare for this. I do not know how to brace myself for the grief that swells inside me, for the terror of watching it all unfold. I thought I had understood the enormity of the task when I first began. But now, with the ark full, with the rain about to fall, I see the truth of it all—how little I truly understand. The sky trembles, and my own heart follows. For every creature I've saved, there are thousands more that will not survive. I cannot save them all. The flood is bigger than any of us. Bigger than me, bigger than the ark.

I close my eyes for a moment, feeling the weight of the promise, the burden of it. I remember when I first received the call. It felt as though the very heavens themselves had spoken directly into me. I remember the weight of God's voice, its quiet certainty that I would be the one to save the innocent, to preserve the life of the earth. But now, it feels as though I stand on the edge of a precipice, waiting to fall into a chasm I cannot see. I am alone in this, though I am not alone. I am surrounded by the creatures, by the promise of salvation, but in my heart, I am still standing at the edge of a great unknown.

I think of my sons, their faces shadowed by doubt, by the weight of my vision. How can they understand? How could they? I've asked them to believe in something that no one else believes in, to follow a plan that defies reason. The people outside mock us, their laughter still ringing in my ears, and I wonder if they are right. If we are all fools, clinging to some old myth, some old dream. What if this ark, this plan, is nothing but a folly? What if the waters never come?

But no, I cannot afford such doubts. Not now. Not when the door is shut, and the world beyond is already changing. I must trust in what I've seen, in what I know, even if it defies everything I've ever known to be true.

I cannot help but feel the weight of the emptiness outside the ark, the vast expanse of the earth, once alive with song and now swallowed by silence. The fields, the rivers, the mountains—they are gone now, in my mind, even though they still stand outside the ark. They are gone, because they will be swallowed by the flood. The creatures in here—they are all that remains, all that I can save. And I, in this ark, am both the savior and the witness. I will bear witness to the end, and I will bear witness to what comes after. I will hold the memory of the world in my heart, even as it is washed away.

And still, in the quiet of the ark, I feel the pulse of life. The pulse of hope, even though it is fleeting, even though it is small. I have done what I can. I have built this vessel, this shelter, for those I love, for the creatures I have been entrusted with. And though I cannot save the earth, I can save them. And that, I suppose, is enough.

The storm is here. The flood is coming.

But for now, all I can do is wait. And pray. Pray that I have done enough. Pray that I can bear the weight of this final moment, this final test of faith.

Part 10: The Storm's Approach: A Meditation on the Flood

I stand before the rising tide,
    Not knowing what it means to be.
    What has the sky whispered, soft as guilt,
    In secret, into the soul of man?
    I feel it now, the weight of time,
    The flood that's coming, the endless climb—
    I have been called, but will I rise?
    The earth is dying. The ark—my prize.

The creatures stir behind me still,
    They know the tempest, they sense the chill,
    Yet I, who stand with trembling feet,
    Am torn between the promise and defeat.
    My soul drips with the weight of grief,
    Of knowing this end, beyond belief.
    The heavens loom, a shroud of blue,
    And in their depths, I see the truth.

What is the meaning of this curse?
    This cleansing flood—this endless verse?
    The waters, deep as ancient sleep,
    Shall swallow, drown, and make us weep.
    Yet here I stand with hands still stained,
    With faith so wild, yet strangely waned.
    What gods have whispered this command?
    What fate is this, so vast, so grand?

ALEX TELMAN

The thunder cracks, it calls to me—
    A voice I once knew—now deep, now free.
    But even thunder bends its ear
    To the sound of death and whispered fear.
    The stars have turned their gaze away,
    The mountains bend to night's decay,
    And still the flood will come. It calls,
    The waters rise, and darkness falls.

What is this ark, this fragile shape,
    That holds the weight of all the faith?
    Is it a refuge from the deep?
    Or does it bear a truth too steep?
    I have built it with my heart and hands,
    But now it trembles on shifting sands.
    I knew its purpose once—divine—
    But now I see the flood as mine.

The creatures, they are innocent—
    Do they know their fate, their final scent?
    The lion's roar, the eagle's cry—
    Will they fall to the flood, to the sky?
    And in their eyes, I see my own—
    The hopeless, fleeting seed I've sown.
    For who am I, to stand and save
    When I cannot stop the world's wave?

The rain begins, a gentle sound,
    A murmur soft, that shakes the ground.
    The earth, once lush, now bows to fear—
    What have I done? What brought me here?

THE EPIC OF NOAH

Was it my faith that led me on,
Or was it doubt that lingered long?
For every step I took in trust,
I felt the soil beneath me rust.

And still, the rain begins to fall,
    A thousand voices—one last call.
    The ark, a womb of wood and stone,
    Now holds the weight of God alone.
    But I, a man of flesh and bone,
    Stand wondering if I'm truly known.
    For who can know the weight of sin,
    The drowning heart, the soul within?

I see my sons, their faces pale,
    As rain begins to swell the dale.
    They look to me, but I look not—
    What answers do I have, what thought?
    My faith once sharp, once clear as day,
    Now clouds in sorrow, swept away.
    The flood will come, the earth will weep,
    But will I find my soul to keep?

I cannot answer, not just yet,
    For I am lost, in grief, in debt.
    I built the ark, I sealed the door—
    But did I trust what came before?
    I held my faith as tight as stone,
    But now I fear I stand alone.
    The rain falls faster, the flood will rise—
    Will I drown beneath the skies?

ALEX TELMAN

And yet, beneath the waters deep,
    I feel a stirring, soft to keep—
    A hope, a thread that winds its way
    Through night's great ocean, past the day.
    For in the flood, I see a light—
    A beacon dim, yet burning bright.
    I do not know what it will cost,
    But I will sail, no matter what is lost.

For in this flood, in this great pain,
    There is a truth I can't explain—
    The waters may rise, the world may fall,
    But I am here. I have answered the call.
    The ark may be my final home,
    But in its shadow, I will roam.
    I will endure, I will survive—
    For in this flood, I come alive.

I sit on the edge of the ark now, where the wood meets the stone, looking out over the land, knowing the water will soon rise. The wind carries the scent of the sea, the promise of it. Not the salt you know, the kind that stings and foams, but something darker. Something ancient. I hear the first drops of rain tapping like fingers against the roof, their rhythm soft but insistent, as though they already know the shape of the world to come.

    It's strange, to feel this weight pressing in on me from every direction—this weight of waiting, of knowing. There was a time, not long ago, when I thought I could manage it. I thought that if I built the ark, if I followed the design He gave me, if I endured the scorn of those around me, it would make sense. I thought I would come to a moment when it would be clear. And maybe that moment has come, but it's no more clear than it was when I first received the command.

THE EPIC OF NOAH

The animals are inside, safe for now. My sons helped, though there was something unspoken in the air between us. Something too heavy to name. I couldn't make them understand, not in the way I wanted. They believed, but not as I did. Not with the same weight. I tried to speak to them—about the flood, about the reason—but how do you explain to a man, to a boy, that the end is not coming for them, but for everyone else? How do you tell your own sons that the world they know will soon be erased, not by their hand, but by something far greater?

I looked at them when we finished. They stood there, their backs to me, in silence. A part of me wanted to reach out, to touch them, to give them some last bit of comfort. But it didn't seem right. It didn't seem necessary. They had their own lives, their own paths, their own questions. They didn't need me to hold them together. They didn't need my burden.

I feel it now—the burden. The weight that has followed me from the first moment I heard the voice. His voice, soft and loud, like thunder in my chest. Sometimes I wonder if I heard it wrong, if the wind carried the words with it, twisted them somehow. But no—there's no mistaking it. It was Him. He has always been clear. He has always been true.

I stand now in the ark's great belly, the walls rising on either side. I see the shadows of the animals, their eyes glowing in the dim light. It's strange to be surrounded by them. I've built this vessel to carry life, but it feels more like a tomb. The storm is coming, and I cannot stop it. I could not stop the laughter of the people when I told them. I could not stop their mocking words, their mocking eyes, as they watched me toil on. I could not stop the fear that seized me each time I stepped outside. There were moments when I wanted to turn away, when I wanted to walk back into the house, tell my family that I had been wrong, that the flood was not coming. But I never did. I couldn't. The vision He gave me was too vivid. The flood would come, whether I believed or not.

But now, standing here on the precipice, I question everything. The rains will come, the earth will break, and all that I know will be swallowed whole. But what does it mean? What does this world-ending flood mean for me? For my sons? For the creatures, who have never known what I've known? Will the earth truly be washed clean, or will it be swallowed by the weight of its own sin, its own guilt? There are so many questions, and no answers.

ALEX TELMAN

I try not to look out at the horizon, because each time I do, I see the shadow of the coming waters. I feel them—rising, rising, the waves cresting behind me. I wonder, sometimes, if I could've done more. If I could've done something different. Perhaps if I had told them sooner. Perhaps if I had acted faster, or prayed harder, or had more faith.

But I did. I did what He told me. I did what I was meant to do. And yet, the emptiness that creeps into my chest, this nagging doubt, gnaws at me still. What if I am wrong? What if this is not salvation but the beginning of a great, endless night?

I turn to look at the animals again. I see the lion, the snake, the bird perched on its beam. All of them—silent, waiting, with their own mysteries. Did they know what was coming? Did they feel it? Or were they just waiting too? Waiting for me to lead them? The thought makes my chest tighten.

But I'm not ready. Not yet. The rain falls harder now, a steady drum, rhythmic and relentless. The sound of it fills the ark, and I find it strange how soothing it is, as though it's drawing me back into some ancient rhythm, some forgotten pulse. Perhaps that's why I built the ark. Perhaps it's not just for salvation, but for the very act of building something that can withstand the storm. Maybe that's what He wants—something that stands in defiance of the waters. A sign that no matter what happens, life can endure.

It's hard to believe, though. The world outside, with its laughter, its ridicule, its false comforts, seems so far away now. I want to believe in the promise of salvation. I want to believe that when the flood comes, when the waves crash down, there will be something on the other side. But the question lingers in my mind—What does it mean to survive? What does it mean to be saved, when the cost of salvation is the destruction of everything you've ever known?

I have only one answer: I don't know. And maybe that is the hardest part of all.

But I will wait. As I have always waited. For He has not left me. The rains are falling. The ark is ready. And for now, that is enough.

Part 11: The Flood Begins

The heavens opened wide, a rift in night,
    A wound in silence tore the breath of light.
    The storm began with whispers in the dark,
    A tremor felt, a ripple—then the spark.
    Thunder cracked, its voice the sound of doom,
    As though the stars themselves had met their tomb.

The ground beneath me quaked, its spine did bend,
    The earth itself began to meet its end.
    I stood upon the threshold, staring out,
    And saw the sky descend in shrouds of doubt.
    The first drops fell, so small, then quickly grew,
    A deluge breaking loose—an ocean's view.

I called to my sons, their faces drawn with fear,
    Their hands outstretched as if to hold it clear,
    But words were lost, like whispers in the din,
    For all the world now felt a storm within.
    The ark stood ready, wooden ribs still warm,
    Its promise hollowed by the coming storm.

And then the animals—two by two they came,
    Like shadows marching to a funeral flame.
    The lion, fierce, with his great eyes aglow,
    And lambs as meek as rivers in their flow.
    The birds of air, the beasts that roamed the field,
    With trembling hearts, their fates were all revealed.

ALEX TELMAN

My wife beside me, her face a mask of grace,
    But in her eyes, I saw a darker place.
    The fear, the grief—how could she understand?
    How could she bear the weight of heaven's hand?
    We moved together, silent, through the door,
    As rain began to pour, and then to roar.

The door was shut. The seal was set in place,
    And in that instant, I could see each face—
    The ones I loved, the ones I could not save,
    The ones left standing on the shore to brave
    The waters that now rose like hungry flames,
    A tidal wall that called them by their names.

I held the timber of the ark's last wall,
    And in its grain, I felt the earth's great call.
    Was it the gods or was it fate I heard,
    That urged me onward, driven like a bird?
    I could not turn. I could not stand apart.
    For in my chest, the flood had drowned my heart.

My sons, my sons, their faces grim and white,
    They turned to me, their voices filled with fright.
    "Father, father, tell us what this means,"
    They asked, as waters licked the grassy greens.
    But what could I reply, when in my mind,
    The truth was drowning, drifting, left behind.

The ark began to creak beneath the strain,
    Its boards now groaning like a soul in pain.

THE EPIC OF NOAH

The storm outside beat louder with each breath,
Each crash a promise of the world's swift death.
My heart, it quaked, it trembled in the gale,
And with each wave, I feared our fragile sail.

The waters rose like vultures circling high,
    And all I knew, I wished to question why.
    But then my eyes returned to what we'd built,
    The ark now floating, scarred but still unspilt.
    And there, upon the deck, my family stood,
    Together, bound by faith and ancient blood.

The rain came in torrents, filling the sky,
    Like rivers washing mountains low and dry.
    The wind became a voice of ancient grief,
    A howling cry that sought no word of relief.
    And all around, the world began to spin,
    As if the heavens knew the sins within.

I heard the cries—the distant, dying sound
    Of voices lost, of men who stood unbowed.
    And in their eyes, I saw my own despair,
    A mirror bright, yet touched by death's cold stare.
    How many hearts had I failed to save?
    How many souls would meet the flood's dark wave?

I turned away. My eyes began to close,
    For there was nothing left but what I chose—
    To walk in silence through the rising tide,
    And trust in God who called me to this ride.

ALEX TELMAN

But though the storm raged fierce, and still it howled,
I held my faith, though every promise fouled.

The ark, it rocked, as though to claim the sky,
    As heaven reached to meet the earth in sigh.
    And then my sons, their voices filled with dread,
    Spoke in the dark: "Father, is it now we're dead?"
    But I—what could I say, what truth was clear?
    That all that once had stood, was now severe.

And in that moment, as the storm did rise,
    I felt it in my soul—the last demise,
    The end of all that lived upon the land,
    The final word from God's unyielding hand.
    Yet still, I stood, unbroken, deep in prayer,
    For all that had been given, all that shared.

Through crack and cry, through every crash and roar,
    I called to Him, though I had asked before.
    But now I knew—though heaven's door was shut,
    I had no place to go, no door to cut.
    The flood had come. The end had swallowed all,
    And I stood here, alone within its thrall.

The rain, the wind, the thundering sky did break,
    As though the world itself would bend and shake.
    But in the ark, the creatures pressed with care,
    As if to share the fate they'd come to bear.
    And in that moment—then, beneath the flood,
    I held my faith, my family, and the blood.

THE EPIC OF NOAH

The waters rose, but still, we carried on,
    Through storms and silence, we endured till dawn.
    No man's voice could break the pounding sound,
    But here I stood—amidst the flood's cold round.
    And though the earth was lost to waves and tears,
    I prayed my sons would rise above the years.

The heavens split. The sky, a torn cloth, Tears poured down, not as droplets but as rivers, Descending with an ancient rage, An anger that swelled, that roared, and shuddered, Crying out through the trembling earth, That had waited—waited through seasons of silent promise— For this one moment when its breath would break.

    The earth, as though it had borne too much weight, Gave up its strength beneath my feet. Cracks split open like old wounds, Fissures bleeding water from the deep, Gushing in fountains, rushing up, Grabbing at the soil, at the trees, Like hands desperate to pull it all under.

    I stood in the ark, trembling in its wooden bones, The animals pressed close, some quiet, some restless, The air thick with the smell of earth and panic. The thunder cracked—its voice the sound of breaking worlds— As my sons, their faces pale as ash, Climbed aboard, each step a whispered prayer, Each breath the last in a silence that screamed.

    The wind howled and swept the earth into chaos. I turned once more to see the land we had known, To see the fields where we had planted, where we had walked, Now vanishing, submerged in the wrath of the waters. And I felt it—deep within, as though a hand gripped my heart: The weight of what was happening.

    The people—oh, the people—did they hear it too, The sound of the world ending? Did they hear the cry of the skies opening wide And know, as I knew, that they were too late?

    I remember the faces—their laughter, Their disbelief, their eyes mocking the sky, But now those faces had turned to the water That rose up like an army, Unstoppable and fierce, Pulling, pulling everything in its wake.

ALEX TELMAN

My family huddled together, fear rising like the tide. My wife's voice trembled as she called my name, But I could not answer her. Could not explain the ache in my chest. Could not explain how the world had grown so small, So distant, as if I had been lifted from it, A man in an ark, watching his world disappear.

The door closed with a finality that rang in my ears. A sound that echoed with the weight of years— The years of warning, of toil, of silence— And the seal of fate that had been pressed upon us. I could not look back. I could not look forward. There was only the rising, the swelling waters That pushed against the ark's walls, testing its strength.

I could feel the earth beneath me tremble, And as the flood began to take hold, I saw the first tears in the sky, Falling not like rain, but like a veil That covered the world, and the world went dark.

I looked at my sons. They were silent now, No longer mocking, no longer defiant. The reality had descended upon them too, The weight of the task we had carried— Not just to build the ark, not just to save the creatures, But to stand as the last witnesses of a dying world.

We drifted. That's what we did. We drifted. The storm pressed in from every side. The cries of creatures filled the ark, The low growls of the lions, the soft calls of the birds, The frantic flutter of wings. And I stood, not as a man but as a vessel For something greater than I could understand, A bearer of faith and of sorrow, A keeper of life, and of the end of it.

I wanted to shout. To cry out. To ask Him why. Why had I been chosen for this? Why had He asked me to witness this destruction, This cleansing fire that would leave nothing behind But the bones of a broken world?

But the rain kept falling, and the wind kept howling, The thunder cracked like a whip, and the ark Moved slowly forward, borne on the waters As I held on to my faith, to the promise He made. Though I could not see Him, I knew He was there— There in the storm, there in the rising tide, There in the very heart of the flood, Where the waters came to wash the world clean.

My heart pounded in my chest, and my hands Gripped the sides of the ark, and I felt my faith Shudder like a leaf caught in the storm. I had never known fear like this. Never known what it was to stand on the edge of the world, And feel it turn beneath me.

THE EPIC OF NOAH

The flood was here. The flood was here, and I— I was just a man, alone in the midst of it. My family was beside me, yes, but even they, Even they did not know what it was to carry this weight. I looked out through the small window of the ark, And all I could see was the endless wall of water, Rising higher, swallowing the world, And I closed my eyes, not because I could not bear to see, But because there was nothing left to see.

I held my breath and waited, As the ark rocked, as the flood rose higher, And the voices of the earth became drowned in the sound of the waters. And I wondered—if I were to die here, in this ark, Would the earth remember us? Would it remember what we had done?

But the waters came. And there was nothing else.

Part 12: The Submersion and Hope for Renewal

I stood upon the water's boundless edge,
    Where sky and sea in endless union pledge.
    The world had sunk beneath the angry tide,
    Yet in my heart, the flame of hope did bide.
    I gazed upon the wreckage of the earth,
    A land once full of life, now lost to dearth.

The mountains disappeared, their peaks no more,
    As waves upon the shore did crash and roar.
    The rivers swelled, their veins now pulsing wide,
    And in their depths, the memories did hide.
    No more the winds would whisper through the trees,
    No more the sun would warm the earth's cold seas.

Yet here I stood, the last of all who knew,
    The weight of love, the burden deep and true.
    For in this flood, this cleansing, harsh and wide,
    A silent promise rose upon the tide.
    A word not spoken, but felt in the soul,
    That from this death, a birth would soon unroll.

The silence echoed through the drifting span,
    A stillness deeper than the heart of man.
    No cries, no sound, save for the ark's soft sway,
    As if the earth itself had ceased to pray.
    The land was gone, the creatures lost to night,
    Yet still I felt a flame, a distant light.

THE EPIC OF NOAH

The ark, our refuge, floating in the deep,
    Did carry us through waters vast and steep.
    And yet within its heart, I felt the ache—
    A longing for the world we could not wake.
    For every life now lost beneath the sea,
    A thousand voices whispered unto me.

I prayed for them—the ones who did not hear,
    The men who laughed, who turned from love and fear.
    But in their fall, I saw no hate nor blame,
    For we are dust, we burn and leave no name.
    The flood was God's, and I had walked His way,
    A servant loyal till the break of day.

And in the night, I saw a distant star,
    A glimmer faint, yet calling from afar.
    The moon, it rose, a silvery soft glow,
    And though the world was drowned, I felt the flow
    Of hope that ran as steady as the tide,
    A promise whispered in the waters wide.

I thought of life that once had filled the air—
    The birds, the beasts, the fragrant trees so fair.
    Yet here we float, alone in endless space,
    While waters blind the earth's forgotten face.
    The stars above, like watchers, still remain,
    Yet what of them? Do they still feel our pain?

ALEX TELMAN

I turned to those who shared this floating cage,
    My sons, my wife, our faces marked with age.
    The flood had made us all, in time, the same—
    United now, we burned with love's pure flame.
    And though we had no land beneath our feet,
    The ark's embrace made all our hearts complete.

I saw my sons, and in their eyes I knew,
    That though the world was gone, we'd start anew.
    The waters whispered softly, as the night
    Wrapped us in tender arms, away from sight.
    For even in the deep, I felt the spark,
    A light that whispered, "Hope will find the dark."

In every wave, in every drop of rain,
    I felt the pulse of life that would remain.
    For though the earth was buried 'neath the sea,
    From death there comes a new eternity.
    The flood would pass, the ark would rest again,
    And life would bloom as flowers after rain.

I prayed that what was lost might find its way,
    That what had died could rise with the new day.
    For though the past had been erased by flood,
    The future held a promise born of blood.
    I held my breath, I waited for the dawn,
    The light that whispered, "Carry on, carry on."

The earth was torn, but in its tear I saw,
    A future bright, a seed that God had sown.

THE EPIC OF NOAH

I knew the ark would rest upon dry land,
And in that place, the world would make its stand.
And though the grief I felt would never cease,
In time, I knew, the world would find its peace.

And so I stood, and watched the flood retreat,
    And in its wake, the heavens felt complete.
    For though the earth was drowned, I knew inside,
    That from its death, a greater life would glide.
    The waters fell, the ark began to sway,
    And with it, hope arose from night to day.

I spoke to those beside me, soft and clear,
    "Behold, the world will rise again, my dear."
    And in those words, I felt the weight of time,
    A sacred truth, a whisper so sublime.
    For death may come, and floods may wash it clean,
    But from the depths, a new world shall be seen.

The ark began to glide upon the tide,
    And in my soul, the seed of faith did bide.
    The flood would pass, the earth would rise once more,
    And in its bloom, all things would be restored.
    The end was but a turning, swift and wide,
    For in its wake, the dawn would rise and glide.

And so I waited, as the waters cleared,
    My heart still heavy, yet my soul revered.
    The world had died, but hope was born anew,
    In every drop, the promise shone through true.

ALEX TELMAN

The ark, my vessel, carried us through pain,
And in the light, we'd rise again—again.

The flood is not a sudden thing. It doesn't crash upon you with the force of a tidal wave, though it does drown all that is familiar, all that you have known, until nothing remains but the vastness of the water. It is a slow, inevitable thing—an unfolding, like the opening of a great and terrible flower. The rising tide is only the beginning, and it stretches on and on until your soul becomes as vast as the flood itself, until you feel that you are no longer in control of the world, no longer its master, but simply a passenger on the river of fate.

I had built the ark with my own hands, with the sweat of my brow and the ache in my bones, and yet now, at the cusp of the flood, it feels as though the ark is not a refuge but a prison. The world outside is lost, drowned beneath the endless expanse of water. The stars that once dotted the heavens like jewels have been swallowed by the endless cloud, and the land—so solid, so unyielding—has been turned to a shifting sea of oblivion.

Inside the ark, it is quiet. My sons have gone silent, their voices now but distant echoes. We are all here, in this place together, bound by God's command and our own trembling faith. The animals are restless in their pens, pressing against the walls, eager to flee but unable to. They, too, know something is coming. They sense it. They feel it in their bones, in the shifting air that heralds the storm.

And then, at last, it begins.

The first raindrop falls, a solitary bead of water, hanging in the air like a prayer before it strikes the earth. And then another. And another. The rain falls as though it cannot be stopped, each drop a hammer striking the earth, a message that no one can ignore. The waters begin to rise. The ground, the earth that once held us all steady, now gives way, turning to mud and ruin beneath our feet.

I stand at the edge of the ark, looking out into the rising flood. The panic is creeping into my chest, but I push it away. I cannot afford to feel it. I cannot allow myself to be afraid. There is no place for fear in this moment—only the

THE EPIC OF NOAH

silence of God, the certainty of His will, the knowledge that I have done what I was commanded to do.

But still, my mind trembles. I turn to look at my family, huddled in the corners of the ark. My sons are as still as I am, their eyes wide, their hearts heavy with the weight of what they know is coming. My wife, who has never questioned my faith, looks at me with a kind of sadness that I cannot understand. What is it, I wonder? Does she mourn for the world that is slipping away from us, or does she mourn for me? For the burden I have taken upon myself, the weight that has crushed my spirit? I cannot tell. I do not know. All I know is that the flood has come, and we are trapped within it.

The waters rise higher. The ark lurches, the sound of wood creaking beneath the strain. The earth is gone now. The sky is gone. All that is left is this water, and the stillness of the world beneath it. I know, deep in my bones, that there is no turning back. There is no undoing what has been done.

I think of the people I knew—the men and women who laughed at me as I built the ark, who mocked me when I spoke of the flood, who turned away when I begged them to repent. I think of their faces, their laughter, their disbelief. What will become of them, I wonder? Are they drowning now? Are they crying out for mercy? Or have they already been swallowed by the deep, lost to the waters that rise with such inexorable force?

The flood is not a punishment. It is not vengeance. It is a renewal. A washing clean of the earth, a chance to start again. But how can I know that? How can I believe that, when the water is rising and the world is dying? When my soul is heavy with the grief of all that has been lost?

The animals are restless again, their sounds filling the air like a chorus of panic. The ark shudders beneath their weight. I place my hand upon the wooden boards, feeling the steady pulse of life that moves through the ark. In that moment, I know that I am not alone. God is with me, with us, with all of creation. And though the flood is terrifying, though it threatens to undo everything I have known, I know that it will pass. The waters will recede. The earth will dry. And in the silence that follows, life will begin again.

I look out once more, past the rain, past the endless sea. There is nothing left but the flood, nothing but the water that holds us all in its grasp. But in the distance, through the rain, I see a glimmer of light. A spark of hope, a reminder that the end is not truly the end. That even in the darkest moments, there is a glimmer of the future waiting to emerge.

I cannot see it clearly, but I know it is there. I know that it is coming.

And so I wait.

The flood is not over yet, but it will be. The earth will be reborn, and with it, hope. There is nothing left to do but wait, and trust that God's plan will unfold, that what He has promised will come to pass. The storm is here, but the dawn will come. The flood will pass, and in its wake, a new world will rise.

Part 13: Isolation on the Ark

I.

The world is silent now,
its voice swallowed beneath a sea of grief.
The ark, a floating womb in endless night,
sways with the rhythm of ancient winds.
I walk its length, my steps a dull echo
on the wooden floorboards,
each creak a prayer that breaks
against the vast silence.
We are all that remains—
the last remnants of a forgotten world,
drifting in a sea of waiting.

II.

My sons do not speak as they once did.
Their voices have thinned, like the air
above the water, strained and brittle.
Japheth, ever the dreamer, stares out,
his gaze lost in the void beyond the hull.
Ham is consumed by shadows,
his silence an open wound that festers beneath
his eyes, once so full of fire.
Shem keeps to himself,
as he always has,
his hands busy with tasks
that do not ease the weight
settling on his chest.

III.

My wife—

her face is a mask,
a porcelain mask, cracked at the edges,
her tears long dried beneath the salt of the flood.
How many days, how many nights,
have we spent together in this solitude?
I do not know.
Time has folded upon itself,
a page forgotten in a book too old to turn.
She will not look at me.
She will not speak.
I wonder if she still believes—
in me, in this promise,
in the hope we once had.

IV.

And the animals—
the creatures of every shape and size—
press themselves against the walls,
their eyes wide with confusion,
their instinct at war with the stillness
of this man-made world.
How strange it is,
to be surrounded by so much life
yet feel so terribly alone.
I wonder—do they too mourn?
Do they too remember
the sun and the earth?
The call of the winds and the rivers?

V.

I hear the scratching of claws on wood
as a rat scurries across the floor.

THE EPIC OF NOAH

The birds make their mournful song—
a noise that breaks against the silence,
its echo lingering long after.
I have not seen a sky in days,
have not felt the earth beneath my feet
in what seems like an age.
Only the water remains,
an endless flood of grief and doubt.
And the rain,
it has not ceased.
It never stops.

VI.

I have wondered many things in the night.
I have wondered what it means to lead,
to carry this burden,
this weight that grows heavier
with each passing moment.
I hear the sounds of my family,
their restless movements in the dark,
but we are strangers now,
bound by a fate none of us chose.
I wonder, too—
will we ever speak of this again?
When the earth is dry,
when the flood recedes,
will we return to each other
or will we be forever changed?

VII.

I have not spoken to God.
Not in days.

ALEX TELMAN

Not since the rain first fell
and the waters began their rise.
I no longer know what to say.
What do I ask of Him?
What can I ask when I have seen
the depths of His will,
the breadth of His power?
I feel so small,
so insignificant before Him now.
And yet He is with us,
still and always.
I feel Him in the creaking of the boards,
in the low hum of the ark's motion,
in the stillness that presses down upon us all.

VIII.
  This is the weight of faith,
  this endless waiting,
  this journey across the abyss,
  with no land in sight,
  no end to the storm.
  We are suspended,
  caught in the space between
  what was and what will be.
  In the void, we must find our way.
  In the silence, we must learn to speak again.

IX.
  I see now how the flood is not just water,
  but time—
  a great torrent of moments
  that cannot be stopped.

THE EPIC OF NOAH

Each drop,
each wave,
is a piece of the past,
a memory drowned beneath the weight
of its own destruction.
And yet, even as it pulls us under,
it cleanses.
It makes room for something new.

X.

There are days when I wish I could return
to the beginning—
when the world was still full of light,
and the earth was whole.
But I know better than to dream of such things.
For the flood has come,
and it has carried all things with it.
There is no going back.

XI.

We have no choice but to wait,
to wait for the waters to find their way,
for the ark to find its place in the world again.
What is left for us,
except to endure?
What else is there
but the passing of days
and the aching, constant hope
that someday,
somewhere,
we will see the sun again?

XII.
    And yet, there is something in this isolation
    that begins to shift.
    At first, it was suffocating—
    this loneliness that clung to us like a second skin.
    But now,
    in the quiet,
    I feel it—
    the stirring of something deeper,
    something that lives beneath the weight of the flood.
    Perhaps it is hope,
    or perhaps it is just the heart's ability to survive
    even in the darkest places.

XIII.
    I think of the earth,
    how it once held us,
    how it once sustained us.
    And I think of the future—
    the world that awaits beyond the flood,
    a world still unknown,
    still full of possibility.
    The ark is a coffin, yes,
    but it is also a womb—
    a place where life waits to be reborn.

XIV.
    And in this space,
    this moment,
    I see the horizon through the dark,
    a glimmer of what is to come.
    The flood will end,

THE EPIC OF NOAH

    and we will step onto the dry ground,
    and the world will begin again.
    We will be the ones to walk it.

XV.
    And though it feels endless now,
    though the weight of the flood bears down
    with each passing hour,
    I know that we will survive.
    We will endure.
    And in that endurance,
    we will find our strength again.

And so, we wait.

The waters have risen.

    There is no more sky, no horizon.

    The world is submerged, a murky expanse that stretches beyond the edge of my sight. I've become so accustomed to the swaying of this ark that I no longer distinguish the waves from the pulse of my own heart. The silence is an echo that I carry, everywhere I walk, everywhere I go. We have been sealed inside, enclosed in a vessel that was once a thing of promise. Now it feels like a tomb. The creatures shuffle, restless, unsettled by the same weight that presses down on my chest.

    I hear the rats scurrying in the dark corners, hear the restless cries of the birds in the distant holds. My sons, once so full of life, have retreated into themselves. Japheth, the dreamer, still stares out from the narrow windows as if he could glimpse the world beyond. But there is nothing out there. Nothing but the ceaseless waters. His eyes, once alight with hope, have dimmed to match the gray sky. He speaks less now, his words brittle, like the wood we've walked across for days. His silence is louder than any words.

Ham, ever the skeptic, drifts in a haze of frustration. He has become distant, unreachable. I see his shadow pass by the walls, hear his footsteps dragging. There is anger in him, a bitterness I cannot console. He does not understand the necessity of this. I can feel his gaze when it passes over me—disbelief mixed with accusation. I am a man of action, and yet I am as lost as he is. Perhaps more so. There are days when I too question what it all means.

Shem is quieter than ever. He works without complaint, fixing things that need mending, attending to the animals without a word of protest. His actions speak more than his silence. He has always been the one to carry the burden with grace, to hide the pain behind a steady face. But I know that even he feels it—the crushing weight of what we have become. I see him, sometimes, sitting alone in the darkest corners of the ark, his eyes vacant, as if he is searching for something just beyond his reach. It pains me to watch him, but I cannot reach him. None of us can.

And then there is my wife. Her silence is the heaviest of all. She who once filled our home with laughter now hardly speaks, as though words are a luxury we can no longer afford. I know she is afraid. I know she fears the days to come, fears what we are becoming, what we have lost. I want to speak to her, to hold her and tell her that it will end, that we will find land again, but I cannot find the words. There is too much distance between us now, a chasm deeper than the waters that swirl outside our walls. Her eyes never meet mine anymore. Her gaze is fixed on some unseen horizon, one that I cannot follow. I wonder, sometimes, if she sees the world as I do—unrecognizable, drowning, lost.

What are we waiting for? What is the end of this journey? The storm has not ceased; the rain does not stop. It has been so long now, I cannot recall a day without it. The waters have stolen the earth from us, stolen the very ground we once stood upon, and left us adrift in this place between worlds. How much longer can we endure this isolation? How much longer can I look at the faces of my family and not feel the weight of their disappointment? Their disbelief? Their sorrow?

I look to God. I do. But it is different now. The silence in my heart is the same silence that stretches across the waters. What have we done to deserve this? What have they done? My sons, my wife, the world we left behind—it is all so much greater than I can carry, than I can understand. The flood was supposed to cleanse, to purge, but what has it cleansed? I look at my sons, at my wife, and wonder—are we the ones being tested? Are we the ones who must prove ourselves? We have lost everything, and yet I still hear His voice in the quiet of the night. I still feel His presence, even in this weight. But it does not make the waiting any easier. It does not make the silence any less suffocating.

I cannot tell them how heavy this is. I cannot explain the sorrow in my chest. The weight of what is lost, what is gone. I cannot speak of the loneliness that comes from being the last of a kind. The last of a hope that feels foolish now. There are days when I wish I could turn back, when I wish I could undo all of it. But there is no undoing. The flood has come, and we are adrift, bound to it, swept away by it.

The animals—the creatures we saved, the ones that will repopulate the earth—are restless too. They sense it. They feel the shift, the tremor of something greater than their instinct. They are as lost as we are. They wait, each of them pressed against the walls, each of them carrying the burden of what they do not understand. The birds are quiet now. The lions no longer roar. Even the fish in their watery depths are stilled, as though the waters themselves have swallowed their voices.

I wonder if they feel it too—the weight of survival. The cost of it. For what is life, if it is not lived freely, on the earth that was made for us all? How can we go back? How can we walk upon dry land again, knowing what has been lost, knowing what we have destroyed?

But I do not know the answer. I do not know what is waiting on the other side. There is only this—this ark, this journey that stretches on, without end, without certainty. I look at my family, each of us adrift in our own way, lost in the storm. But still we remain. Still we wait. Still we breathe.

I pray, but the words are thin, no longer the confident calls I once made in the quiet of the fields. Now my prayers are whispers. My faith is stretched, pulled tight like a string before it snaps. And yet, I wait. I wait, because there is nothing else to do but endure.

I do not know what the flood means. I do not know what it is to survive it. But I do know this: we are still here. And that, perhaps, is enough.

Part 14: The Chaos of the Flood

The heavens split, a voice like thunder rolled,
    The mountains crumbled, and the oceans swelled,
    A world undone, no mercy to behold,
    A cosmic cleansing in the tempest's hell.
    The flood surged high, a storm without reprieve,
    The ground consumed beneath the sky's harsh grieve.

I stand in silence, though the world outside,
    Shatters in its wrath, a cosmic tide.
    The ark, our shelter, groans and creaks in pain,
    The weight of water pounding on the frame.
    I hear the moaning of the beast and bird,
    Their cries, though muffled, break my heart in thirds.

The chaos swells, it echoes in the night,
    The flood's fury roars—a primal fight.
    The cries of those who drowned, the earth undone,
    The waves rise higher, swallowed by the sun.
    I cannot help but hear it all—inside—
    The dark, the endless sea, a broken tide.

The wind is sharp, it howls through every crack,
    And with it, loss, a shrieking panic's track.
    I hear them—lives that flicker in the deep,
    Whispering to the waters, calling, weep.
    The earth has bled, and now the skies collapse,
    Our hopes and prayers, entangled in the laps.

THE EPIC OF NOAH

How long, O Lord, how long must we endure,
    This endless wrath, this flood that none can cure?
    How many lives must drown, how many fall,
    Before the silence answers to our call?
    The ark is not a safehold from this grief—
    It trembles still, beneath the storm's belief.

The lightning strikes, the thunder rends the night,
    And in the chaos, I feel no respite.
    The world outside is lost, the earth is gone,
    The very stars are swallowed in the dawn.
    I listen close, but all I hear is sound—
    The howling winds that tear the world around.

The beasts grow restless, their sounds fill the space,
    The panic of the storm begins to trace
    Its echoes deep within our very hearts,
    A trembling fear that never once departs.
    The ark is but a cage that holds our shame,
    And yet, its walls are sanctuary's name.

What have we done to make this world unmade?
    What sin is writ that shadows us in shade?
    We did not seek this—no, it came unasked—
    This flood, this purge, this fate we cannot grasp.
    Each wave outside drowns memories we've known,
    Our lives are lost in waters that have grown.

The flood has taken all that once was light,
    It took the earth, the moon, the stars, the night.

ALEX TELMAN

There is no place for solace, no refrain,
The flood has swallowed joy, and all is pain.
Yet still we stay, for what? To see the end?
Or to remain, though all we know will bend?

The storm persists, the walls begin to bow,
    And still we wait. But what awaits us now?
    The world that was is gone, consumed by strife,
    A barren wasteland to reflect our life.
    The ark holds us, but does it keep us whole?
    Or merely shield our bodies, leave our souls?

The cries outside are like a call to war,
    And all I know is gone, is lost once more.
    We cannot see the world that was before,
    We only hear the wind and thunder roar.
    Our minds are frail, the burden far too great,
    And I, a man, confront my final fate.

Noah's heart trembles, for it sees it clear—
    The world's rebirth, the death that men must fear.
    And in this hour of darkness, endless flood,
    I see the tears of earth, its beating blood.
    The sky is split, the heavens torn apart,
    And I—no different—feel it in my heart.

This storm—its weight is all-consuming still.
    The ark is small, the waves are steeped in will.
    I feel the dread of earth beneath the tide,
    The cries that rise with fury, deep inside.

THE EPIC OF NOAH

The flood has come, and now we see the price—
A world erased, a lost, descending ice.

The silence in the ark, a hollow cry,
    The emptiness outside, where none dare fly.
    The chaos rages on, yet here we stand—
    The ark, a cradle built by God's own hand.
    We cannot leave; the storm is all around—
    Our fate is written in the water's sound.

The flood outside, it mirrors all we've known,
    The weight of our transgressions, overthrown.
    The wind it howls, the storm it does not cease,
    The world outside is drowned in endless grief.
    I stand upon the ark, alone with all—
    The waters rise, the great destruction's call.

And yet, within this chaos, I still pray—
    For after night, the dawn must surely stay.
    For though the flood may rage, we must endure,
    And know that after storm, the earth is pure.
    The ark, though frail, shall carry us through this,
    And on the other side, we will find bliss.

The world is unrecognizable. I close my eyes to the memory of it—a distant dream. The earth, the sky—gone. In their place, a churning mass of water and fury. The winds scream as if the heavens themselves are tearing apart. The rain pounds, relentless, as if every drop is a hammer smashing at the brittle bones of creation. The ark, once a sturdy promise, now groans beneath its burden. My body, too, groans. I feel the weight of it all in my bones, my very marrow, as if the flood itself is inside me. But it is not just my body that trembles. My soul shakes. Every moment, the air vibrates with fear. I hear it in the whispers of the animals—the frantic scuttles of paws, the soft whimpers from the birds, the deep, sorrowful roars from the great beasts. They know it too.

I have always been a man of faith, or so I believed. I built the ark with that faith, trusting in a promise that came to me from the heavens, a promise that I would save those who could not save themselves. I trusted that this was my purpose. And yet, now, as the floodwaters rise, my faith falters. The storm outside is too fierce, too all-consuming. I cannot see beyond it. The waters, endless and unforgiving, blot out the sky. The sound of them fills my ears, drowning out every other thought. The ark is a fragile thing. A floating speck in an ocean that feels as though it will swallow everything—everything and everyone.

I look out from the narrow windows of the ark, my hands pressed against the wood, and I cannot see where the earth ends and the sea begins. I hear only the cacophony of destruction—thunder cracking the heavens open, lightning flashing like a blade across the sky. The roar of the wind. The pounding of the rain. The shrieks of the animals. I cannot tell if they are afraid of the flood or of something worse, something far deeper. I cannot tell if their fear is the same as mine.

I think of the world before. The green hills and the quiet valleys. The stillness of the early mornings, the way the sun would kiss the horizon. I remember the laughter of my sons, their bright eyes full of dreams. How long ago that seems. Now there is only the darkness of the flood and the endless despair. The animals are silent for moments at a time, then their cries come again—sharp, guttural, piercing the silence like knives. It is as if they too sense the enormity of what is happening. And what is happening? What is this? This chaos, this reckoning? Is this punishment? Or is it something else, something I am not meant to understand?

The flood is not just water. It is a force—an undeniable presence. It sweeps over everything, consumes the world whole. How can I stand here, amidst all this, and still believe in the promise that God spoke to me? I feel the weight of that promise now, heavier than any of the timber I used to build the ark. Was I wrong to think I could carry it? Was I wrong to think that I was the one chosen for this task?

THE EPIC OF NOAH

I hear my sons. They are trying to comfort the animals, trying to bring order to the chaos inside the ark, but their voices shake. They are afraid too. I can see it in their eyes when they glance at me, waiting for me to say something, anything, that will give them hope. But I cannot. The world outside is unraveling, and I feel like I am unraveling with it. My mind spins in endless circles, my thoughts a whirlwind of confusion and doubt. I cannot bring comfort to them when I do not have it myself.

The flood is not just the waters outside. It is inside me too. The fear, the sorrow, the guilt. Did I do enough? Did I build enough? I look at my sons and wonder if they will remember me. Will they think of me as a father who protected them, or as a man who condemned them? I wonder if they understand the weight of what we've done. We built this ark—yes. But what if it isn't enough? What if the flood does not stop? What if the world we knew is gone forever, swallowed by the depths?

The flood is both a destruction and a rebirth, a cleansing of the world. And yet, I wonder if I can survive the very thing that was meant to save us. The earth is being remade, but in the midst of it, all I can feel is the loss.

And still, I do not ask why. I do not dare. There is no time for that. The world outside is fading, collapsing under the pressure of the storm. I know this is not the end, though it feels like it. There is something waiting on the other side. There must be. I close my eyes and let the sound of the storm wash over me, trying to find some semblance of peace amidst the chaos.

I think of the promise God made to me, the promise to save the creatures, to start anew. But how can I think of beginnings when all I hear is the end? The flood has come, and there is no denying it. The world is drowning, and we are in the midst of it. I want to scream, to tear the walls of this ark apart. But I know, somewhere deep inside, that this is all I can do now.

We wait. The ark creaks and sways in the storm. The air inside is thick with the weight of everything. The flood is outside, but it is inside too. It is in my heart. The water rises, and I do not know how long I can stand it. How much longer can we endure this?

But we will endure. I do not know how or why, but we will. I feel it in the depths of my bones, the truth I have carried with me since the moment I first heard the voice of God. And though I cannot see beyond the flood, I know that we are not lost. Not yet.

ALEX TELMAN

I do not know what lies ahead. I do not know what the world will look like when the storm passes. But I will wait. We will all wait, together. For what, I do not know. But I will wait.

Part 15: Moments of Deep Reflection

I stood upon the ark, amid the storm,
    A vessel bound by the will of God,
    And yet, a churning tempest stirred within,
    As though the flood had reached my heart's deep core.
    I heard the waters pounding at the wood,
    But could not silence what surged in my mind—
    The flood was not just of the world, but me,
    For doubt, once quiet, now rang out like thunder.

I remember, in those early days,
    How faith was a mantle, light as air,
    A gift from the heavens, smooth and full,
    Like a river's flow, steady and unbroken.
    But now, as the waters rose and curled,
    That faith seemed heavy, like iron chains.
    The ark rocked and groaned beneath its weight,
    And so did my soul—what was once so pure,
    Now rattled by doubts and questions that came,
    As though the storm outside had birthed them,
    Filling my heart with cold, unanswerable grief.

God spoke to me once, a voice so clear,
    He called me to save His creatures, all,
    But now I wonder, with my hands in prayer,
    How does this destruction fit His plan?
    How can I stand as the flood devours,
    When the promise of life now seems so distant?
    Was I right to build, to trust in His voice,
    When the world drowns beneath a weight so cruel?

ALEX TELMAN

And the animals—why do they cry?
    They know, as I know, the weight of the storm.
    They wait in the ark with eyes wide in fear,
    Hoping for salvation, but none can speak.
    We are all in the dark, struggling to breathe,
    Wrestling with shadows that dance on the water,
    Each whisper from the deep echoes my doubt—
    Is this judgment, or mercy, or something worse?

I cannot ignore the cries of the world,
    The drowning voices that rise in the night,
    Familiar sounds now lost beneath waves,
    And it grieves me, more than any wind.
    Why do the innocent suffer, the weak drown?
    The earth quakes and swallows its children whole,
    And yet I, chosen, untouched by the flood,
    Stand here, locked in the silence of fate.

My mind drifts to that moment in the beginning,
    When God spoke, His words like a vow,
    A covenant of grace, a promise of life—
    But what is grace when the world has drowned?
    I held the weight of His words in my chest,
    But now, the weight is unbearable,
    It drags me down, and I fight to rise,
    Fighting the pull of despair in the flood.

I did not ask for this burden, no,
    Yet I accepted it when His voice called.
    I did not question, I did not speak,

THE EPIC OF NOAH

For the call was pure, and my faith, too.
But now, in this endless night of rain,
I feel my faith beginning to erode—
The ark shakes, and my heart shakes with it,
The floodwaters claim both earth and belief.

I look to my sons, their faces pale,
    They do not understand this war within me.
    They cling to the hope of the promise,
    But I am trapped in a struggle far deeper—
    A wrestling match that none can see.
    My faith was once a bright, shining light,
    Now it flickers, wavering like a flame
    Caught in the wind, unsure of its place.

What is faith when you cannot see the way?
    When every horizon is drowned in darkness?
    When the cries of the world surround you,
    And the weight of salvation feels like a curse?
    What is faith when you are left alone
    With only your thoughts and the endless storm?
    Is this faith, or is it a desperate hope—
    A hope that will not drown with the earth?

The waters rise, and I rise with them,
    Fighting, clinging to the promise,
    But what is the promise when all around me
    Is lost to the waves? The flood is not just the world—
    It is inside me, in my heart, my mind.
    I am drowning in the silence of God,
    And yet I know He is with me still—

ALEX TELMAN

Somewhere, in the depths of the storm,
There is a light, a truth I cannot touch,
But I hold to it, for it is all I have.

The ark creaks, the flood groans,
    The world is a vast, empty sea,
    And I—no longer sure of my strength—
    Cling to the hope that this is not the end.
    For how can it be? How can it be
    That this journey, this test, is final?
    God's promise endures, even in the dark,
    Even when I cannot see through the rain.
    I will wait, though my heart trembles.
    I will wait, though the world breaks around me.
    The flood is here, but it will not last.
    It cannot. It will not.

Faith is not the absence of doubt,
    But the strength to endure it.
    And though the ark may sway and crack,
    Though the world may disappear beneath waves,
    I will hold to the covenant—
    The promise He made, that I still carry.
    For even in this silence, even in this pain,
    I believe that a new world will rise,
    And we, we will rise with it.

The storm began as a whisper, like a secret passed from one corner of the universe to the next. But now, as I sit here, the wind has grown into something monstrous, a beast whose breath is full of death. Every gust roars like the cries of the broken world below us. The ark sways with each gust, groaning like a tired

THE EPIC OF NOAH

man carrying a burden too great to bear. I too groan, though no one can hear it but the wood beneath my feet and the creatures who share my loneliness. We have been locked in this floating prison for so long now. I no longer know how many days have passed since the flood began. Time stretches thin and useless, like the very air I breathe.

    I try to hold on to the faith that once came so easily to me—like sunlight, like a gentle wind on a warm day. I was chosen. I had heard the voice of God and obeyed, without question, without hesitation. But now the waters rise around us, and I am not so certain. The faith that once felt like a steady foundation now seems fragile, a flickering candle in the midst of an eternal night. The ark, this monstrous thing, is both my salvation and my prison. It is filled with the cries of animals that I once thought were part of God's perfect design, but now their sounds grate against me. I hear the lions growling, the birds flapping their wings in frustration, the restless pacing of the elephants. They all sense the weight of the destruction, the end of all things. They know what I know, but they cannot voice it.

    I sit on the floor of the ark, staring at the endless blackness outside. The flood is not just the world. It is me. It is inside me, clawing at my insides like a storm that cannot be calmed. I feel the rising panic deep in my chest. The panic that starts as a whisper but soon spreads until it fills every inch of my being, and all I can hear is the pounding of my own heart.

    The waters outside are relentless. They do not care for the creatures inside or the men who built this vessel. They know only one thing: to rise, to cover, to destroy. I have seen the world change in ways I cannot understand. My hands tremble when I think of it—the world, the people, the cities that once bloomed with life, now swallowed by the flood. I know what is happening is right. I know that God spoke to me, and I obeyed. But what is the cost of obedience when the whole world must drown to make way for something new? What is the cost of salvation when it comes with such destruction?

    I wonder, sometimes, if I could have said no. If I had stood firm and said, "No, Lord, I will not build the ark. I will not save these creatures." Could I have done that? Or was it always going to be this way? Was this flood always meant to happen, and I, like a puppet, was only here to play my part?

    My mind wanders to the faces of those I knew before this—those who laughed when I spoke of the coming storm, who mocked the very idea that something so catastrophic could ever happen. They did not know. They could not know. But I knew. I knew because God spoke, and I heard. I have always been a man of faith, but faith is not always easy. Sometimes it is a burden heavier than the ark itself.

I wonder if they saw me as a fool. If they looked at me as a madman who heard voices and built an impossible boat on dry land, who preached of a flood that no one believed would come. Now, I hear their laughter in the silence of the ark. I hear the mocking words of those who did not listen. I wonder if they are gone now, lost to the waters. I wonder if their last thoughts were of me, of the man they scorned.

But I cannot think of them now. I cannot think of anything but the weight of the task I was given. The weight of this ark. The weight of my family's eyes, who look at me with something akin to fear. They do not say it, but I feel it in the silence between us. The silence that stretches and fills the spaces in my heart. They do not know how I wrestle with myself. They do not know how deeply I question the purpose of this flood.

And yet, when I close my eyes, I see God's face. I remember His voice—soft but clear, like a gentle rain. He told me to build the ark, to save the creatures, to save my family. And in that moment, I knew I had no choice. I had to obey. And I did. But now, as the storm rages, I wonder if I am truly saving them, or if we are all simply going down with the ship.

The rain falls, steady and unrelenting. It is not the rain that frightens me, but the silence in my heart. The silence that fills the ark when the animals grow quiet, when my family sleeps, when I am left alone with my thoughts. In those moments, I question everything. What is faith when the world is collapsing around you? What is faith when you cannot see the end of the storm? What is faith when the voice of God seems to have grown distant, swallowed by the storm itself?

I hear the faintest sounds, the groans of the ark as it drifts on the waters. It is a song of mourning, a hymn for the lost. I do not know if this storm will ever end. I do not know if the world will ever rise again. All I know is this: I am here, I am holding on, and I will not let go. I will not let go of the promise, even when it is hard to see, even when everything around me is crumbling. I will hold on, even when the flood is inside me, drowning my thoughts and my soul.

THE EPIC OF NOAH

    I will wait. I will wait for the storm to end. I will wait for the promise to be fulfilled. And I will hold on to the faith that, though I cannot understand it now, God has a plan that I may never know. I will hold on to the hope that this flood is not the end, but the beginning of something new.

    I will wait.

Part 16: Time Passes on the Ark

I stand upon the wooden floor and hear
    The creaking of the ark, a whisper deep,
    A hymn of ages carved by unseen hands,
    A song of life and death that never sleeps.
    The animals below—their breath, their stir,
    Are echoes in a world that knows no time.
    The rain has ceased, the winds have quieted,
    Yet in my soul, the storm rages on still.

I touch the wood beneath me, worn with toil,
    A vessel now for silence and despair.
    For days have bled to weeks, and weeks to years,
    And I, the steward of a broken world,
    Am bound to this eternal drifting place.
    The sun has fled, the stars all turn to dust—
    Yet we, suspended 'midst the flood and sky,
    Must drift as ghosts, our bodies made of bone
    But hearts made stone, entombed in barren hope.

What was it like—before the flood?
    Before the cries of the condemned?
    What were their voices, sharp as fire,
    Shouting warnings in the dark?
    I see their faces in the swirling depths,
    A world erased, and in its place, the waves.
    And yet—
    A twisted root has sprung within my heart.
    I, who built the ark, now question why.

THE EPIC OF NOAH

The ark—our savior—now becomes our tomb.
    A floating grave of beasts and men alike.
    I, the chosen, have saved but spared none.
    A voice I heard, a command to fulfill,
    To save the life that scorned me, scorned my call.
    But now, what is it worth? The blood that flowed
    From cities proud, from lands of sullen men,
    The streets now flooded, drowned beneath the tide.
    Have I saved the world, or merely stalled its fall?

O silent God—how do I carry this?
    The weight of creation, yet none left to see
    What grows from ash, what rises from the depths.
    I have held the line, and now I stand alone,
    A man upon a ship that cannot dock,
    A man who carries all the weight of sin—
    Of man's designs, of all that I have lost.
    I have saved but only what was meant to die.
    For what can grow when all the roots are drowned?
    How can I plant a tree in salt and rain,
    When all that bloomed is swallowed by the flood?

The ark—my burden—how long will it hold?
    The light is dim, and all the world is gone.
    What have I saved, and what have I condemned?
    The beast below, the creatures I have tended,
    Their eyes hold something I can never touch.
    They do not question. They do not ask why.
    And I—who have no voice to give my heart—
    Shall sail forever through the storms of thought.
    Can I, a man, find meaning in this place,
    Or am I fated, doomed, to drift alone?

ALEX TELMAN

The time passes as the water does—
    Silent, unseen, but certain in its rise.
    The ark is filled with all that God has willed,
    But I—
    I am filled with all that I have lost.
    My family sleeps, unaware of this ache,
    And I, their keeper, wear my grief like chains.
    They see the ark as shelter, as a home,
    But I— I see the ruins of a world.
    I see the faces, blurred by wave and cloud,
    And hear the echoes of a land I loved.

I loved it once, but now I know its sin—
    The sin of pride, of wickedness, of hate.
    And yet—what am I, that I should judge them so?
    I, too, have faults—so many faults to count.
    I, too, have faltered, fallen, broken faith.
    Was I not chosen for my own worth?
    Or did I answer simply to obey?
    Am I the hero in this tale of loss,
    Or simply the one who could not turn away?

Each day the weight inside me presses down,
    A weight that grows with every passing year.
    And in the quiet, I hear voices faint—
    Not of the living, but of those who drown.
    The world once filled with sound now speaks in sighs—
    And I, the keeper, bear this sacred toll.
    The ark may carry life, but can it heal?
    Can it restore what never should have ceased?
    And what of me—whose hands have built this ship—

THE EPIC OF NOAH

    Who sails forever on a sea of doubt?

Oh, what am I to do with all this grief?
    To bear the knowledge of the flood's great cost,
    To watch the skies and wonder if the dawn
    Will ever break to cleanse this ache within?
    For even now, I hear the cry of hope—
    Yet in that cry I hear the echoes gone.
    I saved the world, but did it need to die?
    I saved the beasts, but did the trees survive?

And so I stand, the keeper of the ark,
    The keeper of the faith that still burns dim.
    I will not let it die—this fragile flame—
    But I can feel the weight of all I've lost.
    The ark will carry us—through storm and silence—
    But what of me? Who will carry me?

The ark, a cradle now for life reborn,
    But I—who stand upon its endless floor—
    Will never know the world I've left behind.
    Perhaps I will not know it ever more.

As the water's edge recedes to nothing,
    I will face the world in pieces, scattered wide.
    And in my heart, this burden will remain—
    For I have saved, yet all is left to die.

The ark groans beneath me. It has become a part of me now, this vast wooden shell that has been both my burden and my salvation. The days have stretched into something unrecognizable, not quite days at all. Time itself feels suspended in the swell of water around us. I could have sworn that the waves carry the echoes of the world, and sometimes I think I can still hear it. The laughter of children, the chatter of markets, the hum of life before the storm. But the ark is heavy with its silence now, and it is a silence I carry inside me as much as I carry the weight of all the creatures that sleep below.

I remember the moment the rain began, the first drop that broke the stillness of the sky. The earth seemed to shudder in response, and a cold certainty wrapped around me, like a cloak I could not take off. In that first instant, I didn't know if I was afraid or certain. The flood had come, and it had been coming for much longer than I had ever realized. I thought I understood the weight of the task that God had set before me, but now, in the quiet between each creak of the ark, I wonder if I truly did.

I had been the one to build it. I had hammered each nail into place, with hands that bled and fingers that ached, and I had built it for a world I no longer recognized. A world that had drowned. A world of sin, of laughter that meant nothing, of words tossed into the wind with no care, no care at all for what they were. It was a world that had forgotten how to listen, and now it was gone.

But I am not gone. My family is with me. They sleep below in their little spaces, wrapped in the arms of this ark, this thing that keeps us tethered to the notion that we are alive. And the animals—two by two—they move in the dark, their breathing steady, their instincts unbroken by the storm that has claimed the world. But I do not sleep. I lie awake, pressed into this wooden shell, pressing against the walls of this impossible silence, and I think.

I think of the faces of the people I once knew. I think of the children whose hands I once held, and the farmers whose fields now lie under feet of water. The old man who told me the rain would never come, the merchant who laughed at the idea of an ark when he had seen no flood in his lifetime—where are they now? The city, once alive with movement, with laughter, with trade, has become nothing more than a memory. A whisper on the water. I can see it in my mind as if it is still there, the market square empty, the stone streets slick with rain.

THE EPIC OF NOAH

And yet, I think I hear the sounds of it still—beneath the pounding of the waves. The world is a strange place now. The rain never stops, and the wind howls like a thing alive, hungry for what it can devour. I wonder, in these long stretches of silence, if I ever truly knew the world I saved. Or if, in saving it, I have destroyed something more precious than I can bear to know.

The ark was a task I was given. A task I accepted with the blind faith of a man who has nothing left but the will to follow. I built it, yes. But there is no joy in the building now. No pride in it. I feel only the weight of it. A weight that presses into my chest, making it hard to breathe, hard to think. We saved the animals. Yes. We saved them. But what of the people? What of the hearts I left behind? I stand on the deck of this ark, the only place in the world untouched by the flood, and I wonder if this was what God intended. To save a world by drowning it. To make me the keeper of life only to watch it wash away. What do I know of life when the world is drowned in death?

I have been told I am the last of the faithful, the last of the righteous. But what does that mean when there is no world to be righteous in anymore? The flood came. And I can no longer see the purpose of it. What is there to save when everything has already been lost? My faith is shattered, not in God, but in the idea of salvation. In the idea that anything could be saved. We are all doomed. I feel it now, deep inside me. The realization that I will be the last to bear witness to what has been lost. That I will be the keeper of all this—life preserved in wooden boxes, creatures kept in time until it is safe to start again. But what does it mean to start again? Will it ever be the same?

My family sleeps. I envy them. They do not feel the weight that I carry. They do not hear the world collapsing in on itself in the distance. They do not see what I see when I look into the endless dark. The waves have washed it all away. The world I knew. The world that held me. And now it is only me, here, on this ark, floating in a sea of questions.

What will we do now? What will be left of the world once the waters recede? I can still see it in my mind, that first dawn—the light breaking through the clouds, the ground emerging from the depths like a weary child after a long sleep. But what of us? What of me? What of the weight of this life I must carry now? We will rebuild, I suppose. We will start again, but what will it look like? What will remain?

ALEX TELMAN

It is all so silent now, so still. The animals below me are still, even in their cages. They wait, as I wait. And I will wait as long as it takes. Perhaps that is all we are capable of—waiting for the flood to end. Waiting for the land to rise again. But I wonder, when the land rises, what will I see? What will remain of the people I loved? What will remain of me?

Part 17: Reflection; The Waiting

I. The First Day of Silence
    The skies were stitched with clouds, the water's edge a line—
    And here, within this ark, my thoughts begin to wind.
    The animals, their breath like shadows in the deep,
    Are silent now, as if they too have learned to keep
    Their tongues in the still air, their eyes wide, waiting,
    As if the flood might have them too, its hunger baiting.
    Each day drags slow, the ark a womb, its walls so tight,
    I pace the wooden corridors, bathed in the strange light
    Of lanterns dim, flickering as if they know
    That time and tide are never meant to flow.
    The rhythm of my steps is heavy on the floor,
    Each echo cries out for something more.
    The wind outside begins to die, a ghost of sound,
    But deep below, the seas are churning round.
    My wife sits in the corner, knitting still,
    Her hands so gentle, yet her heart is filled with chill.
    I say nothing to her, nor she to me,
    We wait, we breathe, as though we cease to be.

II. The Second Day of Waiting
    A thud against the side—something soft, something strange—
    The ark creaks loud in protest, shuddering in range.
    I grip the rail and feel the weight of earth now gone,
    The land beneath, the grass and stone, the dawn
    That held us all in place, now swallowed whole
    By liquid wrath, by waters on a roll.
    The animals below me stir in their quiet places,
    Some pacing, some sleeping, some with vacant faces.
    I count each one, to mark them safe within,
    Yet know they feel the loss—the loss of all within.

ALEX TELMAN

Each day I rise to the sound of moaning winds,
A prayer on my lips, and on my hands, the sins
Of a world lost, a world that broke the Law—
What have I done, what do I witness, and what do I saw?

III. The Third Day—Noah's Silent Prayer
    Three days now, and the silence has become a weight,
The sky above like iron, heavy with its fate.
I gather thoughts, though they slip from my mind,
I try to pray, but His voice I cannot find.
What is the meaning of this task so long?
Why has He spared me to watch the flood grow strong?
I go to my knees, but no answer comes.
I whisper to the winds, to the tides, to the drums
Of nature's pulse, but there is no reply.
My soul aches for the ground, for the sky.
I long to feel the sun upon my face,
To walk on earth, to rest in a peaceful place.
The animals rest their weary heads,
And I stare into the dark, alone with my dread.
I wonder what it means to hold the weight of life,
What it means to live beyond the strife.
If the world will never be the same again,
Then what of my soul, and where does it begin?

IV. The Fourth Day—A Change of Winds
    The air is different now, more still, more thin,
The ark moves less, its creaks a solemn hymn.
I hear the hooves of beasts, the fluttering of wings,
And know that life, though fleeting, still clings.
But I see the change in every heart below,
The quiet dread that no one dares to show.

THE EPIC OF NOAH

    I try to speak to my sons, to comfort them,
    But their eyes are like glass, empty of light, dim.
    They, too, feel the weight of the waiting,
    The unspoken bond between us—fading.
    I know that they have felt the same as I—
    The hunger for meaning, the unanswered cry.
    Yet in my heart, I know that this is the test—
    To wait, to stand firm, and know we've done our best.
    The flood will recede, as all things must pass,
    And we will rise, though shaken by the glass
    Of a broken world, a world that was once bright,
    Now drowned in the silence of endless night.

V. The Fifth Day—The Sky Begins to Clear
    The winds, though steady, do not rage as they did.
    The waters begin to sink, as if they hid
    The truths of the earth beneath the surface deep.
    But I dare not trust this calm, for it does not sleep.
    I climb to the roof, the ark's highest point,
    And gaze upon the waters, endless as the joint
    Of earth and sky—how they merge, how they meet,
    And all I see is the sorrow beneath.
    The flood is not just water, it is the loss of days,
    The loss of love, the loss of sacred ways.
    I look into the heavens, and I seek His face—
    But the sky is empty, no answer in space.
    What have I done, O Lord, to bring this end?
    How have I failed, and how will I mend?

VI. The Sixth Day—A Question Remains
    And yet the ark still floats upon the tide,
    Though it is worn, its timbers deep inside

Are cracked and splintered—our lives held by a thread—
And I wonder if it is hope that has fled.
I speak to my sons again, but there are no words,
We hold onto each other, tethered by the birds
That sing in the rafters, their songs full of grief,
Their tiny hearts longing for some relief.
The flood recedes, but in its wake remains
A world lost in sorrow, in sorrow's chains.
I watch as the earth beneath begins to rise,
And yet my heart is cold, locked in its disguise.
What do we do when the flood is done?
What will be left of a world once undone?

VII. The Seventh Day—A Rest that Never Comes
    The ark drifts on, but I am adrift within,
    I have followed the call, but what will come of sin?
    The ark groans louder now, as if it knows
    That the flood was not just water, but the shadow it sows.
    And in the quiet, I begin to ask again—
    What will become of us, and when?

The silence answers.

    The ark creaks beneath me, its old timbers groaning with a weight I can't shake. The flood is here. The waters have come and, with them, a silence. The kind of silence that is thick. The kind that swallows all sound, all breath. I can hear nothing but my own heartbeat. It is steady, even though the world around me is coming apart.

    I stand on the edge of the ark, watching the horizon blur into the swelling tide. My eyes strain against the darkness of the storm, but the wind is sharp, cutting through my skin, pressing me down. I could reach out and touch the waters, but I don't. I won't. I know what it means to touch what's lost.

THE EPIC OF NOAH

There is no land left. There's only the stretch of water, endless and cold. I wonder if I'll ever see earth again, if this will be the last thing I'll know of it—the sky and the water, all of it turning into something monstrous. But even as I think this, something in me resists. The idea of a world destroyed, a world that never was and never will be again, feels too vast to understand. I can't wrap my mind around it. I want to scream at the silence but I don't. I am alone, and the weight of it presses down on me, heavier than the flood.

I hear her voice then—my wife, standing behind me. I don't have to turn to know what her eyes must look like: the quiet dread, the same uncertainty. The ark has become a tomb, and we're all inside, breathing in the same stale air, waiting. Waiting for what? For the storm to pass, for the waters to recede? For a promise to hold us up long enough to see another dawn?

"We will survive," I tell her, though my voice sounds hollow. It doesn't even comfort me.

"We will," she agrees, her words thin like the light filtering through the ark's narrow windows.

But I don't know.

I don't know if we will survive.

The animals—each one a puzzle piece in this absurd plan—are quiet now. Their movements sluggish, as though they, too, feel the weight of what's happening. The lion lies near the giraffe, their bodies curled in unnatural ways, a strange peace between them. The birds sit on their perches, wings tucked in close, eyes alert but unblinking. Even the creatures who once roamed wild, who once knew the earth, are at rest, bound by something deeper than instinct.

It's in this stillness that I hear the first crash. It comes like a ripple through my body, a sound like the breaking of something long held, something fragile. I know it's the world outside, breaking apart.

I shut my eyes, willing it away. My heart stutters.

"Do you hear it?" my wife asks.

I nod, my throat too tight to speak.

I know she hears it too. It's the sound of everything dying. The sound of the earth calling back to itself.

I wish I could go to the door and open it, let the flood in. Let it take me. Let it take us all. I can't bear the thought of waiting, the long days stretched out before me, each one more unbearable than the last. How many days will pass before we find land again? How many days before the flood recedes, and with it, the last trace of humanity?

The days blend together. Time, once so crisp and certain, slips away like water between my fingers. I count the hours in silence, and yet each one feels as though it could be my last.

The animals, the only living creatures around us, have become more than companions—they are the last remnants of something I once knew. I wonder if they, too, are aware of it. Are they grieving for what they've lost, or are they content in the stillness? What does it mean for a creature to know that the world is gone? Does it understand what has happened, or does it simply endure, as I must?

I walk among them, each step an echo, a reminder of the world I once knew. I wonder if they feel it too, the absence of the sun, the loss of the earth beneath their feet. Do they sense that something has been stolen from them, that they are caught here with us, bound to this ark, caught in a moment that stretches on forever?

I want to reach out to them, to understand their silent grief, but I can't. I don't know how.

We are all trapped in this storm, together but apart, each of us floating in our own private silence.

And then I think of the promise—the one God gave me when He called me to build this ark. The one He whispered through the storm, the one that has kept me going through all the doubt, through all the mocking voices, through the weight of my own fear. "I will save you," He said, "and your family. And the creatures of the earth."

I cling to that promise now, but even as I do, it feels like sand slipping through my fingers. Can a man stand in the midst of destruction and still believe in salvation? Can I hold on to the hope of a better world when everything around me is falling apart? The flood waters continue to rise, and the ark sways beneath me, creaking in protest.

I don't know how much longer I can bear this. The waiting, the silence, the constant reminder that the world is dying.

But I know one thing: I cannot give up.

I cannot let go of the promise.

Not yet.

THE EPIC OF NOAH

I turn to my wife, who stands silently beside me, her eyes brimming with unshed tears. She is waiting too, waiting for me to lead her, to guide her through this dark, terrible moment.

"I'm afraid," I whisper, my voice cracking.

"We all are," she says, and there is something in her tone that stirs something deep inside me—a reminder of the love we still have for each other, a glimmer of light in the darkness.

I hold her hand, and for a moment, the world feels small again, just the two of us, standing on the edge of everything, waiting. And maybe, just maybe, that's enough.

The ark groans again, and I close my eyes, trying to silence the fear that churns within me. The storm rages on, but for now, I am here. And I will wait.

Part 18: The Search for a Sign

I sent the raven first, its wings wide,
    Sharp like the darkness above the swelling tide.
    It took flight, soared from the ark's high gate,
    Leaving the waters to claim its fate.

It circled the skies, once filled with cries,
    But now only whispers that pass like sighs.
    The raven, unyielding, flew far and wide,
    But returned not, the silence too deep, too wide.

I watched it go, my heart in the flame,
    Wondering if the world would ever be the same.
    The raven, the dark, the emptiness it wore—
    What did it find on that endless shore?
    Perhaps it found a world beyond despair,
    But there was no sign of it lingering there.

Then I called the dove, with feathers soft,
    A creature of peace, of heaven aloft.
    I sent it out with hope in its breast,
    To bring back word of the world's unrest.

The dove, so pure, took to the air,
    Dancing through the wind, a prayer.
    It fluttered, it glided, it searched the skies,
    With silent wings and searching eyes.

THE EPIC OF NOAH

The days went by like days without end,
    Each moment a stretch, a curve, a bend.
    The ark creaked with the weight of the storm,
    The land beneath it, no longer warm.

I stood at the edge, my eyes cast below,
    Hoping for a sign, for a place to go.
    But the dove did not return at once;
    The flood kept rising, as though to announce
    That hope, too, had drowned beneath the waves,
    Lost, like the cries of forgotten graves.

And yet, on the seventh day, just before dusk,
    When the air grew still and the waters hushed,
    The dove returned, with wings so pure,
    And in its beak, a sign so sure.

The olive branch, green and fresh in its grasp,
    A symbol of peace, a promise to clasp.
    The tree that grew in the garden of old,
    A sign that the world could heal, could hold
    Itself in grace, in renewal's light,
    A token that the darkness would take flight.

I wept as I saw the branch held high,
    For it spoke of hope, and of earth's reply.
    A promise had been made, a covenant true,
    That the waters would recede, and life would renew.

ALEX TELMAN

The dove was my messenger, the bearer of truth,
    A reminder of a world reborn, of youth.
    And though the flood still raged around,
    I knew in my heart that hope had been found.

The ark now held not just life, but the dream,
    Of the earth reclaimed, of the sun's new beam.
    And though the waters pressed against the door,
    I knew, at last, what I was waiting for.

The olive branch, so simple, so pure,
    Spoke louder than words, of a future secure.
    It was not the raven, nor the great beast,
    But the dove with the olive that brought me peace.

And so I stood, with heart lifted high,
    Looking to the heavens, to the sky.
    For the dove had spoken, its wings had flown,
    And in its wake, the light had shone.

Now I knew: The flood would cease,
    The waters would rest, and the world would find peace.
    The earth would awaken, and life would begin,
    A cycle of renewal, of hope once again.

I watch the raven vanish into the storm. Its wings beat against the heavy air, like a shadow, dark and unfamiliar, disappearing into the ocean of sky. For a moment, I am left with nothing but the thudding of my own heart, the silence of the ark, and the endless stretch of water below. The raven, I thought,

THE EPIC OF NOAH

would bring some word, some clue about the state of things out there, some shred of reassurance. But no. It circles the heavens, a void between us, before vanishing—lost, or unwilling to return, or perhaps, as I begin to fear, a sign that the world beyond is still as it was before, a world unrecognizable.

The waters have not stopped rising, though they are no longer the furious rush of their first moments. They are quieter now, settling into a relentless, inevitable rise that stretches onward, without mercy. The ark creaks with each wave, groaning under the weight of this vast, unceasing flood. Inside, the air is thick with the smell of animals, their restlessness a quiet, constant hum. The tension, it never ceases. The burden of it—the weight of what is happening—is something that lodges itself deep inside my chest. A weight that will not lift, a truth that will not be understood.

I sent the raven into the wind—my first desperate effort, a wild plea for something I could recognize, something I could hold onto, like I once held onto the ground beneath my feet. But it brings nothing back, only that gnawing absence.

And so, I turn to the dove. There is something softer about the dove. It is not like the raven, with its wild and untamed flight. It is quieter, more deliberate, less intent on exploring. The dove does not need to fly into the fury of the sky to seek the answers I crave; it will find them gently, with patience. I release it with a prayer I do not speak, a prayer so small, so fragile, it might not reach the heavens at all.

There is something about the ark—the way it feels suspended between worlds. It is no longer the place of work and planning. It is a kind of waiting room. The walls seem to press in, the water seems to press up, and yet I cannot feel the earth beneath my feet. I do not know if I ever will again.

I walk the length of the ark, pacing now like an animal caged in its own sorrow. The animals are quiet for the most part, but I can hear their breathing, their movement—there is something too human in it. Something too familiar. The thought of it all being reduced to this—reduced to an ark full of creatures with no understanding of what is happening, to a vessel adrift in a world that has turned its back—makes my chest tighten.

My eyes search the sky again. The dove is gone. I think I have seen the last of it, the way I saw the last of the raven. The silence stretches out between us, a vast chasm of waiting, and still, the waters keep rising, relentless and inevitable. There is nothing left to do but wait. No choice but to endure.

And then, it returns.

At first, I am unsure of it. The shape is faint, a dark speck against the endless gray. I squint, leaning out from the ark's edge. My heart stops beating. I think I see it—the dove. It comes closer, its wings cutting through the air like something sacred. It flies straight for the ark, so sure in its flight, so assured of its purpose.

And in its beak—a branch. Green. Fresh. It glows in the dim light. It is an olive branch.

I stagger back from the edge, a strange warmth blooming inside me, something I have not felt for days, weeks, maybe longer. The dove, the olive branch, they bring something else—something more than hope. They bring the first real evidence I have seen that the flood might recede. The waters will not always rise. The earth will hold itself together. There is a promise here, and though it is small, though it comes from the smallest of creatures, it is enough.

I sit back on the floor of the ark, pressing my hands against my face, trying to understand. The flood is not an end, it is a beginning. This is not the destruction of all things—it is the rebirth of something greater. A new start. A new world.

The olive branch holds more weight than I thought it ever could. It speaks of something that I had lost—something I could not even name until now. It speaks of peace. It speaks of renewal. Of life after death, of possibility after loss. For the first time in so long, I allow myself to feel a flicker of something—relief? Joy? It is fleeting, like the breeze that stirs the dove's wings.

I know the waters have not receded. The earth is still lost beneath them, but something has changed in me. The dove has returned, carrying the promise of the earth's return, carrying the soft, slow promise of peace. This is not the end. This is just the beginning.

I press my hands into the cool wood beneath me. The ark is heavy, but it is holding us. And we are still here. We are still breathing, still living, still waiting for the land to show itself. The dove has shown me a way forward. A way to believe again. To trust again. In something, in anything.

I look to the sky, the olive branch still resting in the dove's beak, and I say nothing. I do not need to say anything. The world has already spoken.

Part 19: The Waters Begin to Recede

The waters, once a monstrous tide,
    Now ebb and wane in endless stride,
    And where the flood had swept the earth,
    There stirs the tremor of rebirth.

Beneath the weight of ancient rain,
    The ark, adrift, begins its claim,
    To find the ground, the solid stone,
    The quiet pulse of earth alone.

The dawn breaks clear upon the sky,
    The sun emerges, bold and high,
    Its golden rays, the first since then,
    The promise of a world again.

The land, now kissed by light's embrace,
    Holds hope within its quiet space.
    The birds once trapped in skyless flight,
    Now spread their wings in morning light.

The dove that brought the olive branch,
    It flies again, a fleeting dance,
    Its wings cut swift through parted air,
    A sign that life is everywhere.

I watch the sky, I feel the earth,

ALEX TELMAN

And know the time for rest is near—
The flood's fierce roar is but a dream,
A memory of a broken stream.

The animals that crowded close,
    Now stir within their pens, morose.
    Yet there's a spark behind their gaze,
    A flicker of a different phase.

The land that once was dark and wide,
    Now opens to the morning tide,
    The trees, their limbs once wrapped in flood,
    Now shake the water from their buds.

The olive branches—trees that stand—
    Are raised against the touch of sand,
    And though the earth still wears its scars,
    A deeper light begins to rise.

My feet now touch the ground once more,
    The ark, like hope, rests on the shore.
    I look upon the world's vast face,
    And see a hollow, sacred place.

The air is still, the world asleep,
    Yet in my heart, the silence seeps,
    For in the stillness, I have found
    The quiet hum of life unbound.

THE EPIC OF NOAH

I see the birds, the beasts, the trees,
    A symphony in gentle breeze.
    The land, once drowned in endless night,
    Now wears the kiss of morning light.

What future lies beneath this sky,
    What promises that time will buy?
    I feel the weight of what has passed—
    The flood that took, the flood that lasted.

Yet in its wake, a road unspun,
    A dawn that rises, and a sun.
    The future, though I cannot see,
    Is bound in all that's yet to be.

The world, reborn from flood and fire,
    Holds in its hands the deep desire—
    To live again, to love, to grow,
    To climb the hills where rivers flow.

The waters rise, the waters fall,
    But in the end, they are but small,
    A moment's gift, a fleeting test—
    A chance for life to be its best.

I stand here now upon the land,
    My feet upon the softened sand.

ALEX TELMAN

The future, though unknown, awaits,
And all of it lies in our gates.

The world is washed, the sins erased,
   The old, the weary, all displaced.
   Yet in this strange, new life I find,
   A seed of hope, a peace of mind.

For all that's lost, there is a seed,
   That in the dark, begins to breed—
   A tree, a flower, a living thing,
   From which the birds will rise and sing.

And so I stand, and feel the pulse
   Of earth, now steady, now at peace,
   The ark, now still upon the shore,
   And wonder what lies here before.

What's left, now that the flood has gone?
   What's left, when all the old is gone?
   The earth has turned, the sun has risen,
   And we—reborn—are born again.

Though I cannot see what waits ahead,
   I know that life will be instead
   A journey we must take, alone,
   Yet side by side—each flesh, each bone.

THE EPIC OF NOAH

So here we stand upon the sand,
    The ark, our witness, strong and grand.
    The flood may rise, the waters fall,
    But life shall spring, eternal call.

And through it all, we shall endure—
    For we are born from waters pure.

The sky is still. The water is still. All of it, stillness, in every direction. I have never known silence like this. The flood is no longer rushing. The roar of it, the crash and splatter of torrents, has faded into a muffled hum. The ark floats now in a world that holds its breath, waiting for the moment when all things will be pulled back into their proper places.

    I stand at the edge of the ark, looking down at the land below, which has not been land for so long. It seems strange now, how we once stood on this earth without thinking, without needing to remember that it could disappear. It seems strange now, how we thought we owned it, how we thought it belonged to us. It has no obligation to us. I know this now. It was here long before we were born. And if it could, it would stand long after we are gone.

    I don't know what this world is anymore. The trees that were once so familiar now feel like strangers. They are different, quieter somehow, though they stand just as they always did. The air, too. Even the smell of it is changed. A thick, heavy smell of something ancient, as if the earth itself is grieving, or remembering, or both.

    And then there is the sun. The sun, after so long, emerges from its dark cocoon. It does not seem like the same sun that burned the earth with its rays before. It is gentler now, casting a light that seems more fragile, less sure of itself. It is as if the sun, too, has learned something. Or maybe it has forgotten.

    I can feel the weight of it in my bones, the weight of all that has happened. The destruction, the loss, the endless crashing of waves against the earth. It presses in on me, this weight. And yet, there is something else there, something

I did not expect: the faintest stirrings of hope. Hope, like a small bird struggling to take flight, uncertain but determined.

I wonder if it is right to feel hope. How can I allow myself this feeling when so much has been washed away, so much has been lost? My mind runs over the faces of the people who drowned. I never knew them well, but they were my people, my family in this great and endless sea of humanity. How could I let myself feel hope when they have perished, when all that they were has disappeared beneath the waves? But the hope is there, pressing its weight on me, like the sun pressing against the horizon.

The ark has become a prison. The silence within it grows heavy as the days pass. The animals grow restless. They know the stillness as well, their instincts warning them that something is not right. I can hear their movements through the walls—scratching claws, soft feathers rustling, the low moan of some distant creature. Their confusion mirrors mine. What are we doing here? Why are we still waiting?

I do not speak of these thoughts to my family. They, too, have been changed by the flood. We speak only when necessary, our words hollow in the stillness. I see the weariness in their eyes, the questions that go unanswered. There is no answer to be found. There is nothing but time. The hours pass in silence, each one stretching into the next. I keep my thoughts to myself, because what else is there to say?

I have sent the raven and the dove. The raven, a symbol of emptiness, did not return. It is as if it understood the hopelessness of the world and did not care to return. But the dove... the dove brought me the olive branch. A small, simple thing, but in it, I feel the echo of a promise. The olive tree, with its deep roots, symbol of peace, of renewal. It is a sign, I think. A fragile sign, yes, but a sign nonetheless. The floodwaters are receding. And though I cannot see the future, there is a flicker of something new, something that may rise from the wreckage. I hold on to that flicker, even as I do not know what it will mean.

In the quiet of the ark, I find myself searching for meaning in this silence. I wonder if the silence is the answer, if there is something in it that I am missing. Perhaps this is how it will be from now on. Perhaps the silence is the world speaking to me in a language I do not yet understand. But it is hard to know for sure. The silence is thick, suffocating, and yet it holds something. I can feel it, deep in my bones. The world is not yet done with us.

THE EPIC OF NOAH

The dove's return with the olive branch—what does it mean? What are we meant to learn from this moment? Is this the first step in rebuilding? Or is it simply a symbol, a temporary relief before the next storm? I do not know. But I hold on to it, because it is the only thing I have left. A small branch, so fragile, so full of promise. It will have to be enough.

I wonder if it is selfish to hope. I wonder if I have any right to feel hope after all that has happened. And yet, I do. I cannot help it. It clings to me, like the sea clings to the shore. It is not a grand hope, not a glorious one. It is small, quiet, like the olive branch in the dove's beak. But it is hope, and it is mine.

Perhaps this is what it means to be human. To hold on, even when the world falls apart. To find meaning in the smallest of signs, to keep searching even when the path is lost. Perhaps that is all we can do, in the end.

Part 20: The Ark Comes to Rest

The ark groans, its timbers weary,
    As if the weight of the world itself
    Had leaned too long upon its shoulders—
    A vessel made of fear and faith,
    Its ribs now cracked with the weight of time.

The waters that swelled for centuries
    Have finally pulled themselves back,
    But the earth remains shrouded, distant,
    A land unknown, washed of its memory.
    No sign of the horizon's edge,
    Just endless gray.

I stand upon the threshold,
    The door heavy in my hand.
    Inside, the animals sleep,
    Their breaths rising in unison,
    A testament to our shared endurance—
    I can hear it, even through the wood,
    A silence that hums, a trembling hope.

The land beneath my feet is soft—
    Not the ground I remember,
    But something more raw, more vulnerable.
    And the air—it tastes strange,
    Not like dust or salt,
    But like a kind of renewal,
    Like the very air is being born again.

THE EPIC OF NOAH

I step into this void,
    Not knowing what lies ahead—
    No path to follow,
    No guide to show the way.
    The sky above me, so vast,
    Could hold a thousand questions,
    But no answers.

The ark's shelter is behind me,
    But still, it whispers in my ear—
    A memory of what was,
    And what can never be again.

I hear the flutter of wings,
    The cry of a bird,
    Somewhere in the distance,
    And I wonder if it's the last cry
    Of something alive,
    Or a herald of what is to come.

The earth beneath my feet is soft,
    And in that softness,
    I feel the pull of something more—
    Something older than the flood,
    Older than me, older than time itself.

The waters have gone,
    But the scars they left remain—

ALEX TELMAN

The scars in the sky,
The scars in the earth,
The scars in my heart.

What is left to find here?
    What is left to rebuild?
    The world has been washed clean,
    But can it be made new?
    Can I make it new?

I take one step,
    Then another,
    The weight of all that was
    Pressing behind me,
    The silence stretching before.

The air is thick with expectation,
    The land trembling underfoot,
    Like a child waiting for its first breath.

The silence is not the end—
    It is the beginning.

What will grow from this barren place?
    What will rise from this sea of grief?

I have no answers, only the ground beneath me
    And the sky above me,

THE EPIC OF NOAH

The weight of my breath in the vastness of it all.

I look back at the ark,
    Now small in the distance,
    Its edges softened by the fog.

In it, I left the creatures,
    The ones that came with me,
    And in them, perhaps,
    A future lies waiting,
    A future I cannot yet imagine.

I do not know if the earth will bloom again,
    If the rain will fall gently this time,
    If the sun will burn us or bless us.

I do not know what tomorrow holds—
    Or if tomorrow will come at all.

But I stand here,
    Breathing in the silence,
    And I hear the faintest pulse—
    A heartbeat in the soil,
    A whisper in the wind.

I do not know what I am to do here,
    But I know I am here.
    And that is enough.

ALEX TELMAN

The ark is gone,
    The flood is gone,
    But the world remains—
    This world, so vast,
    So empty,
    So full of promise,
    And so full of silence.

I place my foot down,
    And I take the next step—
    And I wonder,
    If the ground beneath me will tremble,
    Or if it will hold steady,
    As I seek my place in this new world.

The earth waits,
    And I wait with it.

What now?
    What now?

I look up,
    And I see the sky begin to part—
    A crack of light where there was none.

It is not much,
    But it is something—

THE EPIC OF NOAH

A promise, perhaps,
Or a sign that the flood
Was not the end,
But the beginning of something new.

The first rays of sun touch the earth,
    And I take a breath,
    A long, steady breath,
    As the world begins again.

I walk,
    Slowly,
    Into the unknown,
    Into the waiting silence,
    Into the future that awaits
    Beyond the horizon.

And I know,
    For the first time in so long,
    That the world is not finished with me yet.

It has not forgotten,
    And neither have I.

I don't know how long I've been standing here, the world still so quiet, the air full of a stillness that presses against my chest. I thought the silence would be comforting—after the roar of the flood, after the unceasing pounding of rain, the crashing of waves against the ark. But it's not comforting. It's suffocating.

Like the silence itself is holding its breath, waiting for something, some sign that the world hasn't completely given up.

I should move. I know that. But my feet—my feet feel like they are made of stone, rooted into this damp, strange earth. I'm afraid if I take a step, the ground beneath me will crumble, or worse, that it will open up and swallow me whole. That's what it feels like. Like the earth itself is too tired to carry the weight of life anymore. Maybe it's not tired. Maybe it's just waiting, like I am. Waiting for something I can't understand.

The ark—the ark is a memory now, not something to hold onto. I can still hear the creaking of its bones in my mind, the soft rustling of wings, the shuffle of hooves, the distant murmur of my family. But that was then. That was before the waters stopped rising and everything began to quiet down. I can't look back at it anymore. I have to face this now. This new world. A world that I no longer recognize.

I think about the others—my family, the animals, the people I left behind. I think about the ones I couldn't save. The flood came, and the flood took them all. That's what it feels like sometimes. That I am the last of something, the last of a world that has been washed away. I don't know if that's the truth, but it's what my heart tells me. The flood took everything. The flood took all of them.

I want to shout into this empty air, but the words are too heavy. They're lodged somewhere deep inside me, and I don't know how to let them go. Every breath feels like a question. Every breath feels like it's pulling me deeper into the weight of what I have done, of what I've witnessed. Was it worth it? The ark. The animals. The faith. Was it worth it if it was only going to end like this? Was it worth it if this is the last breath the world will ever take? The silence is too much.

I close my eyes, just for a moment, and I can almost see it—my family, their faces so familiar, so full of life. I can hear their voices. I remember the warmth of their laughter, the way we'd sit around the fire in the evenings, telling stories, trying to forget the world that was falling apart outside. Now it's just me. Just me and the echo of their absence.

I open my eyes. I look around again. There's no sign of life here, no sign of anything. The world is still, as if it's waiting for me to make the next move. I should be grateful, shouldn't I? Grateful that I survived. Grateful that we made it out alive. That the animals made it out alive. But I can't seem to feel it. Not

THE EPIC OF NOAH

yet. Not with everything that's gone. I was supposed to save the world, but it feels like I've failed it instead.

I step forward, cautiously, like the ground might turn against me. The earth doesn't yield beneath me. I take another step, and another, the wet soil sucking at my boots. It feels wrong to be walking on it. Like I don't belong here. This place wasn't meant for me anymore. I wasn't meant to be here. I was meant to save it, but I'm not sure I know how.

What was the point of all this? What was the point of the ark, of the animals, of the waiting? I know what God said—He said it would be a covenant, that He wouldn't destroy the earth again. But I'm not sure I believe Him. Not now. I don't know how to believe Him. Not when the earth is still silent. Not when the world feels like it's still drowning, even though the waters are gone.

I reach for the sky, as if I can hold the weight of it, as if I can pull it back down to earth and make it right again. But there's nothing to hold onto. The sky is empty, stretched too thin. There are no answers up there. I feel something shift inside me, something small and fragile. I don't want to feel it. I don't want to feel anything. But I do.

A bird. A raven, maybe. I saw it before, or thought I did, flying high above the ark. It could have been a sign, maybe. A sign that the world was still there, that life could still take root in this barren place. But I let it go. I didn't want to hold onto any more signs. I didn't want to hope anymore. Hope is a cruel thing. It brings you to the edge and then pulls the rug out from under you, laughing as you fall. I know that now.

But then I saw something else. A flash of white in the distance. A dove. It landed on a rock, so still. For a moment, I thought it was the same dove I had let go before. It was impossible, but there it was. I watched it, heart hammering in my chest. It moved again, and there, in its beak, an olive branch. Green and alive.

I didn't understand what it meant, but it didn't matter. The world was showing me something. A sign, finally, that life could return. That this silence, this emptiness, would not last forever. That something—someone—was still watching over us.

I don't know what to do with that knowledge yet. I don't know if I'll ever be ready to believe it. But it's enough for now. Enough to take the next step.

Enough to put one foot in front of the other. Enough to believe that the world isn't finished with me yet, that it hasn't forgotten me, that it still holds a place for me in its future.

I take another step, the ground now feeling less heavy, less unsure. And I don't know what will come next. But I have the branch in my hand, the olive branch, and for now, that's enough to make me move forward.

Part 21: The Promise of a New World

The sky unfurls, bright in its waking,
    A trembling stretch of blue above the earth,
    A silence broken only by the breath
    Of life reborn—our first, unspoken step
    Out of the ark, our feet upon this soil,
    This place unshaped, raw in its rebirth.
    What are we but ghosts to this great canvas?
    What does the earth expect from us, her heirs?

I look to the horizon, to where the flood
    Has vanished, as though it never was,
    A memory fading beneath the sun,
    Its waters parting like an ancient veil,
    Revealing land anew—no roads, no homes,
    No buildings, no walls to hold us, no songs
    But the wind in the grass, the call of birds
    That scatter through the air, breaking the stillness
    With their freedom, their cries sharp and strange.

I feel the weight of the past shift,
    Its weight not gone, but lighter now.
    The weight of lives lost. The weight of love.
    It lingers, pressing like a hand on my chest,
    Even as the earth beneath me softens
    And the air, scented with newness, fills my lungs.
    Still, I am burdened by what we have left behind,
    The faces of those who never knew the ark,
    The voices of the drowned who now haunt my sleep.

ALEX TELMAN

Yet, here—here we are. Here, standing still.
    The ground beneath my feet remembers nothing.
    Not the flood, not the storm, not the death.
    It waits for us, as though we are fresh to it,
    A first word spoken in a newborn tongue.
    I reach down, touch the earth, and for a moment,
    I wonder if it knows me, if it recalls
    The weight of the flood, the weight of our hope.
    But no—there is only the wind,
    Only the river that has been born again
    From the veins of the earth, carving paths
    Through the land, through the heart of this new world.

My sons are silent, their eyes wide,
    As they look at this earth that is not ours,
    This earth that we must rebuild.
    And I think of the covenant, the word God gave,
    And how it drifts like a cloud over us,
    A promise that stretches from horizon to horizon.
    The rainbow arcs in the distance, a sign,
    Its colors melting into the blue—
    The first gift of hope, hung high above us,
    And it tells me, despite the years of rain,
    That this world will never again be undone.

God speaks then, His voice low and steady,
    A whisper that trembles through the air.
    "You, Noah, and your sons—this earth is yours.
    I give it to you, to tend and to keep.
    The earth will bear fruit, the sky will give rain,
    The wild things of the earth shall fill the air,
    And you will be the shepherd of this new world."

THE EPIC OF NOAH

I tremble at His words.
    To be the shepherd of such a vast and empty world—
    It is an honor, a burden, a responsibility
    That stretches beyond the limits of what I know.
    And yet, it is a gift I cannot refuse.
    I feel the weight of it settle deep within my bones,
    As the sun rises higher, casting shadows long,
    And the promise begins to take root within me.

Then God speaks again, His voice like thunder
    But full of a strange, quiet peace:
    "This is the sign of the covenant I make
    Between Myself and you, and every living thing,
    That I will never again send a flood
    To destroy the earth. The rainbow will be your sign,
    A token of the promise I give you this day.
    Whenever you see it, remember: I am with you,
    And I will never again forsake you."

I can feel it now—the promise,
    A pulse deep within the fabric of this new world,
    A promise that binds the earth to the sky,
    A promise that roots us to the soil.
    I look up at the sky, at the rainbow stretching,
    And for the first time in what feels like forever,
    I breathe deeply, and the weight lifts—
    Not gone, but lighter.
    And I understand then, what the earth requires.

It requires our care.

ALEX TELMAN

It requires our hands to till its soil,
Our voices to raise in song, to praise the beauty
That has been hidden beneath the flood.
It requires our hearts to hold it close,
To tend it, to guard it, to love it
As God has loved us.

And so we begin again,
    Not as masters, but as stewards—
    Not as conquerors, but as caretakers,
    Learning the language of the earth once more,
    Listening to the whispers of the wind,
    The songs of the creatures that now roam free,
    The gentle flow of rivers winding through fields,
    The rustle of leaves in the trees that stand tall
    Like sentinels guarding the future.

I take my sons by the hand,
    And together, we step forward.
    Not sure of the path ahead,
    But knowing that we walk in the light
    Of a covenant that stretches beyond us,
    A promise that binds us to the earth
    And to each other.
    And I feel, for the first time,
    That the weight of the world
    Has shifted from my shoulders,
    That the burden of its loss
    Has been lifted in the rising of the sun.

The world is reborn in us,

THE EPIC OF NOAH

And we, in turn, are reborn in it.
As the earth stretches out before us,
A land of promise, of potential,
We take the first steps into it,
With open hearts, with faith anew,
And with the hope that, perhaps,
This time—this time—it will be different.

The silence when the ark came to rest was the most unnatural thing I have ever felt. It wasn't the stillness of the earth, but the weight of absence, as if something was missing from the very fabric of being. The floodwaters had receded, but they took with them a part of the world I had once known. The earth itself seemed to breathe in, holding its breath, unsure of what it had just witnessed. How strange it is, to find a world that no longer knows you. To step out of a vessel that has held you, your family, and every living thing you could salvage, only to face the raw truth that the world you once knew is no more.

I stand at the entrance of the ark, my feet touching earth again. The ground is soft and new, and yet it feels ancient beneath my soles. The world stretches before me in a way that is unfamiliar, even though I recognize the shapes of the mountains, the outline of the trees. There is something in the air, something heavy, as though it's waiting for me to do something. Anything. But I do nothing. I stand there, breathing, and wonder what this silence will require of me.

The rainbow appears then, so sudden it almost seems like a dream. Its colors arc high over the horizon, stretching across the sky like a promise—a promise I am not sure I am worthy of. But it is real, this rainbow. Its colors vibrate, piercing through the gray of the world I left behind. I feel a shiver run through my body, not from cold, but from the enormity of it. A sign. A covenant. A word that binds the heavens and the earth. And I, I am caught in the middle, standing with my sons and their families, staring up at this phenomenon that is both awe-inspiring and terrifying.

The flood was never meant for me to understand. It was a punishment, yes, but also a purification, and I—who am I to question such things? There is no language for the depth of the loss we've borne. People—neighbors, friends, strangers—I think of them and wonder where they've gone, what they have become. They are gone. And yet, I am still here. What does that make me? I have saved what I could—my family, the animals—but what else was there to save? What is there left in the world to preserve? This thought weighs on me, crushing in its intensity.

God's voice—when it comes—does not feel like a command. It is not an order, but a quiet declaration. I am to be the shepherd of this new world, to tend it, to protect it. What does that mean? I look out at the wilderness before me, the untouched earth, the trees now swaying in a breeze that feels like the first breath of a new creation. It is beautiful, yes. But how do I begin? How do I take on the mantle of the earth itself, to be its guardian when I don't even know where to start?

My family does not speak, not at first. We are all lost in the enormity of the moment. I have to say something—anything. My words come out as a whisper, an attempt to break the stillness.

"We must begin," I say, though the words feel like a lie. We've been surviving for so long, but beginning—what does that look like? How does one rebuild a world that has been broken apart and submerged in water? How does one build from the wreckage of all that is gone?

My sons, each in their own way, take in the new earth before them. They know—of course they know—that there is no going back. The past is gone. And the future, too, feels like a shadow that hangs just beyond our grasp. The world is open to us, but it is empty in its openness. What will we fill it with? And, perhaps more pressing, *how* will we fill it?

I walk toward the place where the rainbow has landed, its end dissolving into the distant mountains. The earth beneath my feet is soft, still damp from the flood, and I feel it—this land, this world, is waiting. Waiting for something to give it meaning again. Waiting for us to learn its language, to understand its rhythms.

The covenant. It is the promise that everything will be different, that the earth will no longer be cursed, that the floodwaters will never again sweep away all life. But it is also the promise of responsibility. God has not given us a gift without requiring something in return. He asks us to tend this earth, to be its

THE EPIC OF NOAH

caretakers, its stewards. We, who were once the children of the earth, are now its parents. The weight of this, too, is almost too much to bear. What if we fail?

The air is heavy with that question, with the weight of what comes next. And yet, I feel something else, too. Something deeper than the fear or the loss. There is a quiet certainty that comes with this covenant. A knowing that this is the work we were always meant to do. To care for the earth, to protect it, to love it. It is no longer about survival—it is about rebirth. About giving this world a second chance, just as we have been given one.

I turn to my sons, and for the first time in what feels like forever, I see their faces without fear. They are not afraid of the future. They are not afraid of the task ahead. There is a strength in them that I have not seen before—perhaps it has always been there, waiting for this moment. For this new beginning.

And so we stand there, together, in the silence of this new world. The rainbow arcs high above us, a sign that the storm has passed, that the worst is behind us. It is not the end, but the beginning of something else. Something I cannot yet understand but must trust. In that moment, I know that it is not about the flood. It is about what we do next. The world is ours to rebuild. And I, for the first time in what feels like ages, feel ready.

Part 22: The Renewal of Faith and the Beginning of the New World

In the quiet morning air, I stood,
    Fingers brushing the new earth—
    A land washed clean, a promise restored.
    The weight of silence hung, heavy,
    Like the dawn itself held its breath,
    As if waiting for something,
    For me to take the first step
    Into the future, into the unknown.

The world was beginning again,
    A new creation, fresh and trembling,
    And I, the last of men,
    The father of what would be,
    Watched the sun's light scatter over
    The desolate soil that once held
    The bones of cities and towns,
    Now silent, as though it too had wept,
    Now dried beneath my feet.

The covenant is no mere whisper,
    But a thunderous presence,
    A word that roots itself in my soul.
    It courses through me,
    Through the pulse of my blood,
    A reminder of both loss and promise,
    A bond unbroken, unyielding.
    The rainbow in the sky,
    That grand, unspoken vow,

THE EPIC OF NOAH

    Is a bridge between my heart
    And all that is left to be,
    And all that must be rebuilt.

What can I do with such a charge,
    To tend and guard this fertile land?
    How do I step into this vastness
    And shape it with my trembling hands?
    The flood has taken so much—
    All that we were, all we knew,
    Swallowed in the water's greed,
    Yet the earth sings now,
    It sings of life, of hope.

I am not the first to hear it—
    My sons, my sons hear it too.
    Their eyes are bright with a new kind of light,
    And they move, they work,
    In the quiet dance of rebirth.
    I watch them, these men I fathered,
    And wonder: Have I done enough?
    Will they know what it means
    To keep the promise I have been given?
    To carry it forward
    To generations that have not yet been born?

What will they know of this flood?
    What will they remember of the wreckage?
    What will they say when the earth quakes,
    When the wind howls,
    When the waters rise again?

ALEX TELMAN

Will they fear as I feared?
Or will they trust the promise,
Trust that the rainbow
Will always come after the storm,
The sign of peace after the chaos?

But I, I still carry the weight—
    The weight of those lost to the waters,
    The weight of the lives not spared.
    How do I tell them of the ones who perished,
    Of those whose names we never spoke aloud?
    How do I speak of their lives,
    When the flood was a roar,
    A torrent that swallowed whole
    Our world, our hearts, our dreams?

The old world is gone,
    And yet the new world hums beneath my feet,
    Alive with the pulse of possibility.
    I feel it in the soil, in the trees,
    In the breath of the wind that curls
    Through the branches of the olive tree,
    Now growing again, reaching for the heavens.

I am a father now,
    Not just to my sons,
    But to all that is to come.
    My hand rests on their shoulders,
    And I know, even in my uncertainty,
    That this is my role, my charge—
    To guide, to protect, to teach.

THE EPIC OF NOAH

I think of my father,
    Of the men who came before me,
    And I wonder what they would say—
    Would they understand this world I have inherited?
    Would they see in it the same promise
    I have been given?

I walk the earth now,
    But I do not walk alone.
    The weight of my children beside me,
    The weight of their futures before me,
    Is enough to hold the heavens steady,
    Enough to see me through.

There are no more questions now,
    No more doubts,
    For the rainbow stretches high,
    A sign of what is and what will be.
    God's promise shines bright,
    And though the world is small,
    The world is ours to shape,
    Ours to fill with life, with love,
    With a new kind of grace.

The earth is fresh,
    The skies are clear,
    And I—though weary—
    Step forward into this world,
    The father of all that is to come,
    The keeper of the promise.

ALEX TELMAN

There will be joy here,
    I tell myself, though the road is long.
    There will be pain, yes,
    But the light will break through.
    The first step is mine to take,
    And in this moment, I am not alone.

This is the beginning.
    This is the world reborn.
    I, Noah, am its steward,
    And in my heart, a new faith takes root.
    The promise is not just a covenant,
    But a song,
    A song that will carry us through
    The winds and the rains,
    The seasons of despair,
    The seasons of hope.

I will remember the flood,
    And I will hold close the promise.
    And with my sons,
    We will build,
    We will restore,
    We will carry this world
    Into its second chance.

The earth is still too soft underfoot. It gives with each step, a reminder that the flood, the waters, have not fully relinquished their hold. In the silence of the world, there is a constant hum—something deep, something that thrums through the very bones of the land. A vibration. Maybe the earth, too, is

THE EPIC OF NOAH

breathing again. I feel its pulse. It is heavier than mine, more ancient. More patient. And I wonder if it remembers, the way I remember the darkness of the waters, the sound of the storm that tore the old world apart.

I stand here, at the edge of what remains, holding in my hands the rawness of what has happened. I was not prepared for this. How could I be? No one could be. A life spent hearing God's voice, and still, when the flood came, I did not know how to stand in it. I did not know how to stand outside of it, either. The ark is gone now. The animals are gone. The noises, the smells—they too have passed. It is only the wind now, soft and carrying something strange. Something that feels like hope. It almost makes me ache.

I have seen the signs. I have heard the covenant that God placed in my soul, branded like fire. And yet, my feet still hesitate, barely touching this reborn earth. It feels too fragile. What if the world shatters again? What if this too is a dream? But I hear God in my blood, and the weight of the promise presses upon my chest, firm and real. The rainbow, the sign, is still there, always in the background of my vision, stretching across the sky as if it were always meant to be.

But I—how can I feel this way? What does it mean for me to stand here? I am not the first man to walk this earth. I was only the last man to survive it. The others—my father, my grandfather, the countless faces I cannot even remember—would they have understood this moment? They knew a world that was tangible. A world with solid ground, filled with voices and laughter and the flickering of fires under the stars. They knew a world that was not broken. But now—what do I know?

The promise was not for me alone. It was for all of us. And yet I feel the weight of it, all of it, like the whole of creation resting on my shoulders. There is no longer a sea to separate us. No longer the great divide between the firmament and the waters. Everything is woven together now—earth, sky, and the breath of man. But where do we begin? How do we start again? The silence of the earth calls out for an answer, but I do not know if I am strong enough to give it.

I can hear my sons behind me, the shuffle of their feet in the soft ground. They are young still, in many ways, though they are strong and able. They carry the weight of this new world in their eyes. Their futures lie in their hands. What will they build with their hands? What will they make of this place that God has given us? Will they know the same suffering that I knew? Will they build it better than I ever could? I wonder, too, if they can hear the hum of the earth beneath them. If they feel the pressure of the air, heavy with anticipation, with a future that only they can shape.

I turn to them. Their faces are bright with the light of something I cannot quite place—something like faith, but different. They are not like me, these sons of mine. I have been the one to carry the weight of the promise. I have been the one to hear God's voice as if it were thunder. But they—how do they see the world now? Do they look at the rainbow and feel the same thing I feel? Do they wonder about the flood? Do they ask themselves the same questions that haunt me still?

There is a part of me that wants to speak to them—to tell them of the flood, of what I saw, of the emptiness that swallowed the world. But the words don't come. What good is there in remembering the flood when we are standing here, in the after? The future is ahead of us, not behind. And yet, I am frozen by the thought that it could all slip away, that the world could slip through my fingers just as easily as the floodwaters swept away everything else. I wish I could give them the answers they seek. I wish I could tell them how to rebuild the world. But I do not know, and I am ashamed of that.

And yet—there is the promise. The rainbow, bright against the sky, arching like a bridge between the earth and heaven. I have seen it. I have touched it in my mind. It is both a reminder and a promise. And I am not alone in this. My sons, my family—they are with me. We are here, all of us, to start again. It is not the earth that will tell us how to begin. It is we who must shape it. We must listen, listen to the land beneath our feet and the sky above us. It will not be easy, I know this. The weight of what we lost will always press upon us. But there is life. There is light. There is a future.

I will teach them what I know. I will teach them of the covenant, of the rain, of the silence that follows the storm. I will teach them of the world we left behind, so that they might understand the cost of the future. But I will also teach them of hope. The hope that God has planted in my heart, deep, unshakable. This world is ours to rebuild. Together, we will make it our own. And together, we will carry the promise forward, into the future. The weight of the world may be heavy, but it is not ours to carry alone.

Part 23: Rebuilding Life After the Flood

I rise from the shadow of the Ark,
    its hollow frame like the bones of some ancient god
    whose body is now gone,
    leaving only the stillness in its wake.
    The land stretches out before me,
    a raw canvas, scarred but brimming with potential.
    The earth is fertile, as it always was,
    but it has forgotten its shape,
    its place, its purpose.

I stand where the waters have receded,
    where the earth's pulse still quickens
    beneath my weary feet,
    and I know this is where I must begin.
    The soil, rich with promise,
    calls to me like an old friend I once knew,
    its scent, its texture,
    its silence that says so much more than words.

I plant my hands into the earth,
    and the soil is warm,
    alive with the memory of things
    that were lost,
    things that must now be grown anew.
    I have nothing but what I carry within me—
    the legacy of survival,
    the promise that God spoke to me
    when the waters rose like great mouths
    ready to swallow all that was good.

ALEX TELMAN

I kneel in the dirt,
    the land trembling under my weight,
    feeling the shift of history itself
    beneath my fingertips.
    The flood may have washed away all that was
    but it has also given birth to something else.
    This world—this fragile world—is ours now,
    mine to shape, mine to mold,
    to place a seed and wait for its growth
    with trembling hands,
    with fear, with hope.

The rain, once a fury that drowned the earth,
    now falls in soft whispers,
    as though the sky itself is afraid of its own voice.
    It touches my face with a gentleness
    that betrays its past violence.
    I look up, the clouds still heavy with memory,
    and yet in their weight is grace.
    It is grace to rain after such a storm.

I call to my sons,
    the ones who stand beside me,
    each of them with hands like mine,
    small hands that will one day plant and build,
    build with the strength of the world we've reclaimed.
    Their eyes reflect a future that is yet unwritten,
    but I see in them the spark of something new,
    something pure.

THE EPIC OF NOAH

The task is great, but we will not falter.
    We will toil, sweat under the sun,
    dig deeper than we ever thought we could.
    I know the soil now,
    I know its hunger for life,
    its thirst for what it has lost.
    And I will not let it starve again.

We scatter seed in the fields,
    wheat and barley,
    the fruit of the earth rising from our hands,
    and I feel the weight of the old world
    slipping away like a skin too tight for the bones beneath.
    We work through the long days,
    knowing that what we sow now
    is not just for us,
    but for all that will follow after.
    For the children who will run on this ground,
    for the animals that will once again fill the fields.

We raise our homes from the earth,
    stone and timber and the bones of the Ark,
    we build as though the flood had never come,
    as though the world had never been torn apart,
    as though the rains that fell could never rise again.
    But we build with caution,
    with understanding that the ground we walk upon
    is still soft,
    still searching for its own strength.

The air, though heavy, carries a new scent,

ALEX TELMAN

a scent of green things rising,
of life that dares to show its face once more.
And in this, I see God's covenant made clear,
not in the rainbow that arcs across the heavens,
but in the quiet persistence of growth,
in the way the earth chooses to rise again.
This is the true promise—the earth will always renew itself,
and so will we.

I breathe the air, and it fills me with the memory
    of all that has been lost,
    but also with the hope of what is to come.
    I am no longer just Noah,
    the one who survived the flood,
    the one who heard the voice of God.
    I am now the father of this new world,
    the gardener of this garden reborn.
    I feel the weight of the task ahead,
    but also the sacredness of it.
    It is no small thing to be chosen for this.
    And I carry it,
    not as a burden,
    but as an offering.

The land is changing,
    but so are we.
    And as we sow, as we reap,
    as we walk this earth again,
    our hands speak in ways words cannot.
    They touch the soil,
    they touch the sky,
    they touch the hearts of those who will come.

THE EPIC OF NOAH

And they know what it means to begin again.
What it means to rise from the ashes
and to be reborn.

This is no simple task.
    The land will test us.
    The storms will come again,
    but we will stand firm.
    We will remember the flood,
    but we will also remember the green things,
    the seeds we planted,
    the things that took root in the soil of our faith.
    And we will hold them,
    gently,
    in our hands.

And when the earth is full,
    when the fields are green and the trees stand tall,
    we will look up to the sky once more,
    and know that it is not just the rain
    that nourishes us,
    but the promise that the earth will endure,
    and we, with it.

I plant my seed in the soil,
    my hands pressed deep in its cool embrace,
    and in this small act,
    I know I am part of something vast,
    a cycle of life that will never cease.
    And when the next storm comes,
    we will be ready.

ALEX TELMAN

We will build again,
and again,
until the earth remembers that it is whole,
until the earth remembers that it is ours.

I've woken again to the land. It's quiet now—quiet in a way that echoes, filling me up with memories of the past and an unspoken anticipation for what comes next. The Ark is behind me, but it feels like the flood is still in the air, still clinging to the corners of my mind, even as the waters recede further each day. My hands are covered in earth and something else—something raw that pulls me toward the soil, urges me to press deeper, to find the pulse that's buried beneath. I kneel. I dig. The world feels like a fragile thing beneath me, as if the earth itself is remembering the weight of what it once bore and will again bear.

There is so much to do. The Ark, hollow and silent, has already begun to feel like a memory, the wood creaking with the ghosts of its purpose. It was a vessel that saved us, but it was never meant to be home. The home I need to create now is different. The home I need to create is made of soil and sweat and the strength of hands that have learned how to rebuild. The sun is lower in the sky, casting long shadows, but I don't mind. There's comfort in this place, even in its rawness, its promise. I've spent too many days in the dark of that wooden shell, breathing in air that never felt real. Now the earth is alive, its silence profound, heavy with expectation.

I turn to my sons—my three, my pride and my fear. They follow me, lifting their hands to the earth in imitation, unsure of their strength but eager to learn. Their eyes meet mine, wide with a curiosity I once knew. They look at me, as though they think I have answers, but I don't. Not yet. The world is too new, too unknown. We're all grasping for something, trying to make sense of what we've just survived. But they are my foundation now. They are my beginning.

We begin to dig. We plant seeds where the earth has been washed clean, where it still trembles from the water's rage. It is strange, feeling the earth's warmth as I work it. As if I am pulling life back from the depths, forcing it to rise again. The soil, soft under my fingers, responds. The seeds take to it, quickening. But there's a hollowness, a strange quiet that fills the space between

THE EPIC OF NOAH

each task, between each movement. I feel the absence of everything that was once. The flood has taken so much. The animals we once saw, the people we once knew, the villages that stood proud under the sky—it's all gone. The wind that used to carry their voices is silent now. The sound of their lives is gone. It is as if the flood took not just their bodies, but the very sound of who they were. I want to scream at the wind, ask it where they've gone. But I know. I know.

Still, we plant. The seeds feel sacred in my palm. With each one, I promise, not just to the earth but to my family, to the memory of the dead, that I will rebuild. We will rebuild. The land is fertile. The sky holds no rage now. The promise has been made. Even in silence, it is made.

The work is endless, it seems. There are no more questions in the air, only the weight of the task at hand. The days are filled with soil beneath my fingernails and sweat on my brow. I look at my sons, the way their young faces are marked with the same determination that once burned in my own heart. They are learning. They are becoming the men who will carry this world forward. I wonder if they will ever know what it is like to look at a world on the verge of destruction. I hope not.

But for now, we have the land, and we have each other.

I see the wind stir the trees in the distance, but it's different now. Not like it once was, when the wind would scream through the flood's fury. No, now it's gentle, hesitant. I close my eyes and listen to it move, feel it carry the first promise of growth. The promise was not in the rainbow—no, it was in the soil that welcomed us again. It was in the steady pulse of life that has not yet learned to be still. The flood may have washed away everything we knew, but the earth—the earth is alive again. I press my hands deeper into it, my body shaking with the effort, with the weight of what is to come.

My faith, like the soil beneath me, is being tested. But it is not broken. It's in the roots of these trees, in the quiet breath of the plants that rise like ancient prayers from the soil. The faith is in the work, in the sweat, in the hands that press into the earth, as if it might open up and swallow me whole. But it doesn't. The earth holds me, like it has held everything that came before. And in return, I will hold it. I will shape it. I will tend it until it gives me the life that is promised. That is the only way forward.

I feel the weight of it. The responsibility. It's not just to my sons, or to my family, but to the world itself. This world, still so fragile, still struggling to rise.

And I feel a pang of something deeper, something like fear, perhaps, but it's not just fear. It's something older, more primal. The flood is gone, yes. But it is never truly gone. It lingers in the soil, in the hearts of those who have survived, in the breath that each of us takes, remembering what came before.

The new world is ours. But it is not yet whole. It is not yet finished. And I stand here now, on the cusp of what is to come, knowing that the future is not written yet. It will be shaped by my hands, by the hands of my sons, by the hands of all those who follow after us. But for now, we wait. We wait as the earth rises again, and as the sun casts its long shadow across the land. We wait, and we work. And in that waiting, I know that the promise is already being kept.

There is hope in the soil. There is hope in the seeds we plant. There is hope in the work, in the faith, in the earth that holds us still.

Part 24: The Lingering Questions

I step into the silence, thick like dusk,
    beneath the weight of a sky untouched by rain.
    The earth stretches wide, soaked in the scent of rebirth—
    yet beneath my feet, I feel the bones of what was lost.
    The flood, gone, but never gone.
    I cannot forget it. I will not forget it.

I stand before a covenant,
    its shape unfurling like a distant cloud.
    God's promise etched across the horizon,
    but this promise—this heavy promise—
    how does one carry it?
    How does one live with the burden of knowing?

The world that is now,
    it is still too young,
    too fragile beneath my hands.
    The new trees seem to shudder when the wind blows,
    as if remembering what it was like
    to have the storm rush through them,
    tearing the leaves and splintering their roots.
    Is that what I am now?
    A tree, growing, but remembering the storm?

I try to walk in the quiet,
    but my footsteps echo too loudly.
    I wonder how I am meant to fill these spaces
    that stretch between the earth and the sky,

ALEX TELMAN

how I am meant to be a man
when everything around me was washed away.
Is there a place for me here,
or have I become only a shadow
of something that once was,
a ghost drifting between the floodwaters?

There is no flood now.
But the flood, the flood lives in me.
It wraps itself around my ribs,
tightens its grip when I breathe.
I remember the weight of the water,
the pull of it,
how the world once seemed to drown
beneath its roar.

Now the silence has taken its place.
And the silence,
it speaks.
It speaks in the rustle of the leaves,
in the stretch of each new horizon.
And in the night,
when the sky seems too empty—
the silence asks me:
How do you live with what has passed?
How do you live with what you have seen?

I listen to the sound of my children's laughter—
it's sweet, but it feels hollow,
like music too far away to touch.
They, too, will inherit this earth,

THE EPIC OF NOAH

but they do not see it as I do—
they do not know the taste of water
that held the death of the world.
They do not hear the echo of voices
that have faded into the flood,
the ones that cried out for mercy
and were swallowed by the tide.

And yet, here we are—
    alive.
    Living.
    What strange thing is this,
    to live with such knowledge,
    such terrible knowing?
    What strange thing is this,
    to stand on ground that was once
    covered in the weight of destruction
    and now walk in the light of a new dawn?

I raise my eyes to the sky—
    and there it is, again,
    the rainbow.
    A sign.
    A promise.
    But I do not feel comforted.
    I do not feel peace.
    What is peace when the storm
    still stirs in your bones?

God's voice echoed in the thunder,
    promising never again to flood the earth,

ALEX TELMAN

    but what does that promise mean
    when the flood has already passed through me?
    How do I rebuild when I know what destruction feels like
    when I know how quickly the world can end?

The covenant is in the air,
    but the covenant is also in the dust,
    in the seed we plant,
    in the work of our hands,
    in the faith we build despite the silence.
    But how do I know what to trust?
    How do I know what is sacred,
    what is safe to hold?

I carry this burden like a heavy cloak,
    the knowing of the flood,
    the weight of the promise that does not heal
    the place where the waters once stood.
    And still I walk.
    And still I plant.

But there are questions,
    always, questions.
    How do we begin again?
    How do we rebuild when the foundation is cracked
    beneath the weight of what was lost?
    How do we live in a world that has
    been drowned and resurrected,
    a world that feels both young and old
    all at once?

THE EPIC OF NOAH

The soil is fertile.
    The trees grow tall.
    But there are roots beneath them,
    roots tangled in the memory of water.
    I wonder if they remember, too,
    the flood that swept them clean.
    I wonder if they ache as I do—
    rooted in the past,
    struggling to stretch toward the future.

And I wonder if I will ever find peace—
    not the peace of the flood's retreat,
    but the peace of knowing that I have survived,
    that I have been given the chance
    to walk through the storm and find myself
    on the other side.
    The rainbow is there, yes.
    But it is not enough to erase the storm.

How does one live with such knowledge?
    How does one rebuild when the past is so present,
    when the flood is still a shadow in the corner of your mind?
    How do we live,
    when we know what the waters can do?
    How do we rebuild,
    when we know what the waters have taken?

I do not know the answer.
    But I walk.
    I walk in the silence.
    And I carry the promise.

ALEX TELMAN

And I hope that one day
I will find a way to make it my own.

The earth smells different now, like it has learned something new, something old. It is softer somehow, as if the flood that drowned the world also made it more pliable, willing to be shaped again by hands that remember the weight of destruction. The earth's heart beats beneath my feet, but mine does not beat like it used to. Something inside me shifts, like an ancient clock that no longer ticks at the right time, but still ticks anyway.

The children laugh. It is strange to hear them. Their voices echo in the quiet air, as though they are calling from some distant place, a place untouched by water, untouched by the flood. They are innocent. They do not know the weight of it. They do not know what it means to live in the ruins of the old world, to have seen the waters rise and feel them fall, to have stood on the edge of everything and watched it disappear. I want to tell them, but I cannot. How can I tell them? How can I make them understand?

The sky, so clear now, so wide—there are days when I look up and expect the clouds to darken again. I wait for it. There is a stillness in the air, a heaviness that presses down on my chest. God has promised that the flood will never come again. The rainbow, that sign of His covenant, arches across the sky, its colors more brilliant than I ever thought possible, but still, in the quiet places of my mind, I wonder. Is this enough? Does the promise of God really mean that I will never again feel the weight of the water on my skin, the taste of it on my lips, the sound of it crashing against the walls of the ark? Or will I always be haunted by it, by the sound of the storm that drowned the world?

I remember the moment when the ark came to rest. The earth had shifted beneath it, and the floodwaters had begun to recede. The silence that followed was not peace. It was an absence, an emptiness. The noise of the storm was gone, but so was everything else. The world was no longer the world I had known. It was something else, something I could not recognize. It is still that way. There are no words for what I feel. There are no words for the way my mind feels after the flood, how it trembles beneath the weight of everything that has been lost.

THE EPIC OF NOAH

I find myself wandering, searching for something to hold on to, but all I find is emptiness. The world is silent, and in its silence, I feel small, alone.

I watch the children as they play. They run across the fields, their voices echoing against the sky, but it is not the sound of joy I hear. It is the sound of something else, something that haunts me. They do not see it. They do not see the shadow that follows them, the shadow of the flood that still clings to me, to all of us. It is in the way the ground trembles beneath my feet, in the way the air feels too thin, as if it is waiting for something. Something more. I feel it every time I breathe. The flood is gone, but it is still here, inside me. I carry it in my blood, in my bones.

What does it mean to rebuild after such a thing? What does it mean to begin again, when the past hangs over you like a storm cloud, always waiting to break? I have no answers. I have only this silence, this vast emptiness that stretches out before me, a land that is both new and old, untouched and broken all at once. The promise that God gave to me, to all of us, it should be enough. It should be enough to ease the burden that presses down on my chest, but it does not. I hear His voice in my mind, but it is distant, muffled by the weight of everything that has come before. I cannot shake it. I cannot shake the feeling that something is missing, something that cannot be replaced, something that was lost in the flood.

The land is fertile. The trees begin to grow again, their leaves stretching toward the sky, reaching for the sun. I have begun to plant, to cultivate the earth, to do what I must to build something new. It is strange to work in the soil after the flood, after all that has been washed away. The earth feels different now, not like it once did, but like a thing that has learned too much. The earth has tasted the waters of destruction, and now, it moves differently. It is not the same.

I do not know how to live in this new world. I do not know how to walk with faith when I can still hear the sound of the storm in my mind. How can I trust in a world that has been undone, in a world that has been broken and remade? How can I trust in myself when I have seen what I am capable of, what we all are capable of? We are not innocent. We are not clean. We are born from the flood, and the flood is in us.

I walk among the trees, and I wonder how long it will take before the flood returns. Will it come again? Will it come for me? I do not know. I do not know how to live with such a question in my heart, how to walk with the knowledge of what has been lost, with the knowledge of what I have witnessed. I look up at the sky, and I see the rainbow again, but this time it feels distant, like a promise that has not yet been fulfilled.

How does one live with such a burden? How does one rebuild after the flood? How does one begin again, when the flood is still a part of you? The answers are not clear. The answers may never come. All I know is that I must keep walking, keep planting, keep working, even when the silence is deafening, even when the world feels empty. I will carry the promise in my heart, though it is heavy, though it weighs on me. I will carry it, because that is all I can do. And I will wait. I will wait for the day when the flood is no longer a shadow on my soul.

Part 25: Noah's Final Reflection

Upon this shore where winds once blew so wild,
    Where torrents raged and tempest furies riled,
    I stand, alone—though not, for here, in mind,
    My family's voices whisper through the wind.
    The Ark is gone, yet in my heart remains
    The weight of waters, those unholy chains
    That bound the earth and swept away the old,
    The ancient sins, the lies, the hearts turned cold.

A thousand voices, drowned beneath the wave,
    The souls who once did mock, the ones who gave
    No heed to warning, scorned the prophets' cries,
    Now silent, still beneath the endless skies.
    But I—by grace, by mercy undeserved—
    I walk this land, where once the soil was swerved
    By flood and fury, all that man had wrought,
    Destroyed in darkness, by a single thought.

The Lord of Hosts, whose hand had stretched the sky,
    And cast the rain to cleanse, yet sanctify,
    Spoke softly then, as we did sail away,
    And vowed His promise to the break of day.
    No more the flood, no more the cleansing tide,
    To wipe the earth of sin and foolish pride.
    The rainbow stands, a token of His word,
    A bond unbroken, by His hand assured.

Oh, blessed covenant, how firm and sure,

ALEX TELMAN

That never more shall chaos, dark and pure,
Defy the order that He called to be,
As God created earth and sky and sea.
Noah's children, born of hope and grace,
Shall carry forth His legacy in place
Of wrath and ruin—now a peaceful stream
That flows from earth to heaven's boundless dream.

I gaze upon my sons, their faces bright,
    Each one a witness to the coming light.
    Shem, whose wisdom, like the stars, will shine,
    Ham, whose courage in the fight divine,
    Japheth, the gentle, with a heart so wide,
    Together bound, by God's eternal guide.
    They walk the earth, the heirs of Noah's name,
    The sons of the promise, free from shame.

Their children's children, generations rise,
    The nations grow beneath the boundless skies.
    The earth now speaks of life and tender grace,
    No more to fear the flood's consuming face.
    But what of me, the man who built the Ark,
    Who saw the storm, who heard the thunder's bark?
    What will I leave, when all my days have fled,
    When silent winds whisper the words unsaid?

I leave this land, this place where life begins,
    This tender earth that bears the weight of sins.
    For though the flood has passed, the heart still weeps,
    And still the promise of the Lord it keeps.
    The rainbow arcs across the sky's expanse,

THE EPIC OF NOAH

A sign of peace, a long and steadfast dance.
Through time, through ages, down from mountain tall,
The covenant remains, enduring all.
The fire of man will burn, and time will pass,
Yet still will stand this holy, sacred glass,
That mirrors truth in every stormy night,
And paints the world in dawn's redeeming light.
My children's children, they will walk in peace,
And all the earth shall one day know release.
For in their hearts, the love of God shall dwell,
A legacy of grace, eternal well.

The flood has passed, the skies have cleared at last,
    And though the storms may come, they cannot last.
    The covenant stands firm, the word of old,
    A promise made, a story long retold.
    So let the winds of time blow ever cold,
    Let ages pass, let wars and chaos roll—
    For in the end, this truth will still remain:
    God's covenant with man, forever reigns.

I, Noah, now have walked my final mile,
    But still my heart beats strong, my soul does smile.
    For in my sons, in them, I live again,
    A living legacy, beyond all men.
    And when the earth has turned to dust and stone,
    The rainbow's arc will speak, and I'll be known
    As one who trusted in the Word of God,
    And walked with Him, though He did strike the rod.

So let the heavens sing their endless song,

ALEX TELMAN

And let the earth stand firm, both wide and long.
My legacy is not in stone or clay,
But in the hearts of those who walk this way.
A flood once swept, but mercy now prevails,
A covenant of life, beyond the gales.
The Lord has spoken, His promise held true—
The earth shall stand, His people, ever new.

Let Noah's name ring forth in every land,
    For I have seen the glory of His hand.
    And though my time on earth is drawing near,
    The legacy I leave shall never fear.
    For through my sons, and through their sons to be,
    The promise of the Lord will ever see
    Its fullness made, its truth forever told—
    A covenant of life, forever bold.

The rain, it falls in my dreams, a quiet rhythm that lulls me toward something unspoken. Sometimes I wake to find it still pounding against the earth, but then I realize—no, it is only the memory of it, the echo of those days when the world was drowned and I, too, was lost in it. I often wonder what would have become of me had it never stopped, had the waters never ceased their ferocious advance. Would I have been swallowed up along with all those who had turned their hearts from God, those who mocked the warning? Or would I, like the earth itself, have been washed clean?

    The silence now is what aches. After the flood, after the promise. Silence. The birds don't sing as they used to. My sons, they laugh and talk, but the words don't settle the way they should. How do you explain to them the weight of what we have lived through, what we have been through? They were children when the Ark closed. Now, they are men—strong, steady, yet so far removed from the terror of that time. It is not the same for them. They have no fear.

THE EPIC OF NOAH

They do not hear the thunder in the distance the way I do. They do not see the shadows of a world that was lost.

I sometimes think of the old world. Not the world before the flood, but the world I had imagined it would be, the world that was supposed to remain. When the Ark set sail, there was a part of me that believed we would find land, yes—but not just any land. It would be a land untouched, untouched by the corruption that had grown among men, a place where, perhaps, we could begin again, in peace. But this land we have found—this land that stretches out beneath the rainbow, this land where we build and sow and raise our families—feels, too often, like a place we have yet to truly know.

And yet, the sky above, it promises me. I look up, and I see the arc of color—a sign, a mark, something both simple and grand. The rainbow. The covenant. The promise God gave to me, to my family, to all of humanity, that the earth would never again be consumed by water. And I believe it. I do. I must. But there are days—most days, really—when it is so difficult to reconcile what I have seen, what I have lived through, with the world that stands before me now. The land is quiet, yes. But is it peace, or is it just the calm before something else? Another storm? Another wave of darkness, larger and more terrible than the last?

I think of my sons often—Shem, Ham, Japheth. How strange they are to me now, how distant. They were children then, running through the Ark as the waters rose, as the roar of the storm drowned out everything else. I remember their voices, the way they would call to me, ask me questions I could never answer. "How long, Father?" they would ask. "How long until we can see the earth again?" And I, knowing the answer, could never speak it. How long? I didn't know. None of us knew. We were at the mercy of something far beyond us, something that could not be fought with strength or will. Only faith.

And now I watch them grow into men, each of them carrying a burden I did not want for them. They are not the children who once played in the shadow of the Ark. No, now they are the men who must rebuild the world, who must give it new shape, new life. And how do I tell them the truth? How do I explain to them the weight of what was lost, what I lost in the flood? I try to speak of it, sometimes, but they cannot understand. They cannot know the depth of the waters, the endless reach of it. I cannot make them understand the quiet roar in my chest that has never quite ceased.

ALEX TELMAN

I remember the moment when God spoke His promise to me—when He placed His hand upon my shoulder and told me the waters would never again drown the earth. I remember the power of it, the weight of those words, and the stillness that followed. I thought I had heard the sound of the world ending, the cracking of time itself as the flood waters rose. But now, now, I hear the sound of something else, something quieter. The sound of the earth being remade, one small step at a time.

But I know the truth. I know the peace is not in the absence of the flood. It is in the promise that the flood will not come again. That the earth will not be swallowed. That there will be no more water to erase all we have built, all we have loved. The rainbow speaks of this promise, of hope, of a new beginning—but it does not erase the past. It does not undo the terror, the despair. It does not make the memories of those days go away.

The days of the flood, I will carry them with me. Even now, when the earth seems still, when the land stretches out in the quiet of morning, I can feel the weight of it. I can feel the echo of those waters, the endless pull of them. The Ark was a place of salvation, yes. But it was also a place of terror, a place of waiting. I have never been the same since then.

And so, I wait again, but differently now. The world is different now. I see my sons building homes, raising children, planting seeds. They look to me for guidance, for wisdom. And I give it. But there is a part of me that wonders—what do they know of the storm? What do they know of the destruction that once came without warning, without mercy? They carry the world on their shoulders as I once did. But it is not the same world. It cannot be.

Still, I watch them. And I wonder what they will make of it all. Will they remember? Will they see the rainbow as a sign of hope, or as a reminder of what could happen again? I do not know. But I know this: it is not for me to decide. It is not for me to make them understand.

I will leave my legacy in the work they do, in the lives they build. My name, my story, will not be written in the earth itself. It will be written in their hearts, in the choices they make, in the families they raise. That is all I can ask. That is all I can hope for.

And when the time comes for me to rest, when I lay my head down for the final sleep, I will know that the flood is behind me, that the storm has passed.

THE EPIC OF NOAH

The rainbow will still arc across the sky, and I will know that God's promise has been kept.

But what of me? What of the man who once saw the end of the world and chose to trust in God's mercy? I am nothing but a man, a father, a vessel for the story that has been told. But I hope, I pray, that in the end, I will be remembered not for the flood, not for the destruction, but for the faith that carried me through. The faith that still carries me now.

About Alex Telman

Alex Telman is a globally recognized spiritual healer, author, and one of the country's most read poets. With over 45 years of experience, he has dedicated his life to helping individuals break free from negative energies, trauma, and spiritual blockages. His transformative work has empowered a diverse range of clients, including celebrities, business leaders, educators, and everyday individuals, guiding them toward emotional well-being, personal growth, and spiritual fulfillment.

From an early age, Alex demonstrated extraordinary abilities to perceive and remove harmful energies and entities, a gift that first emerged when he was just three years old. This rare talent led him to study with psychic masters across the globe—Afghanistan, France, Sweden, Israel, England, and Australia—each recognizing his unique gifts and helping him refine his craft.

THE EPIC OF NOAH

In addition to his healing practice, Alex has practiced as a barrister, teacher, university lecturer, and small business owner, offering a well-rounded perspective on healing that combines spirituality with practical action. He is also an accomplished author, whose writings inspire and uplift readers by exploring the depths of human emotion and the power of self-healing.

Through his sessions, Alex has helped countless individuals overcome emotional turmoil and reclaim their lives. His work transcends cultural and geographical boundaries, offering profound healing to those in need. His mission is simple yet powerful: to guide people back to their authentic selves, helping them live with purpose, peace, and fulfillment.

With a career built on compassion, wisdom, and deep spiritual insight, Alex remains a beacon of hope for anyone seeking to overcome their struggles and wanting to step into a life of clarity and joy.

Other Titles by Alex Telman

Non Fiction

Entity Possession: Eliminate Your Negative Energies
Congratulations! You're Still A Mess
Mindshift: Change Your Life in 4 Days
Think Like a Modern Guru
Mastering Hypnosis: Complete Step-by-Step Manual, Case Studies, and Sample Scripts
From Cursed to Cured: 100 True Stories of Healing from Curses
Connecting to the Afterlife: a how-to guide
Your Journey from Death to Rebirth
Empower Your Sundays: Unlocking Inner Strength for a Resilient Life
The Truth Behind the Creation Story: A Journey Through Reincarnation
Practical Mentalism in a Nutshell
Reprogram Your Mind in a Nutshell
Meditation in a Nutshell
Alex Telman in Quotes

Fiction

Jackson King: Psychic and the VIP Delusions
A Happy Death
One Life, Half Lived
Down and Out in Byron Bay
40 Flash Horror Stories

Epic Sagas: In Their Own Words

The Epic of Mary
The Epic of the Apostles
The Epic of Moses

THE EPIC OF NOAH

God Speaks
Jesus Speaks

Poetry

Legends and Lessons: 36 Myths Unveiled
Telman: The Complete Sonnets 1974-2024
Telman: The Complete Haiku 1974-2024
Echoes of September 11
Homeless in New York
Burning Echoes of Time
From Dawn to Dusk: the life cycle in sonnets
Eternal Echoes: The Tapestry of Time and the Unseen
Snapshots of People I Have Never Met
A Measure of Time: The Eternal Voyage of Self
Ashes of Verses: Poems Burned But Not Forgotten
Reflections on Solitude: A Poetic Journey Through The Lonely Mind
Your Friendship is a Museum
Whispers to Bella

Don't miss out!

Visit the website below and you can sign up to receive emails whenever Alex Telman publishes a new book. There's no charge and no obligation.

https://books2read.com/r/B-A-YBSCC-FZGUF

BOOKS 2 READ

Connecting independent readers to independent writers.

Did you love *The Epic of Noah*? Then you should read *The Epic of Moses*[1] by Alex Telman!

Discover the Untold Majesty of Moses' Journey

In *The Epic of Moses*, embark on a breathtaking journey through the life of one of history's most iconic figures—a man chosen by God to lead a nation from the chains of bondage to the edge of the Promised Land. This epic poem brings to life the trials, triumphs, and eternal struggles of Moses, exploring not only the incredible feats of leadership and courage that defined his life but the deep, personal battles of faith, doubt, and destiny he faced along the way.

What is it like to hear the voice of God calling you to greatness, even when you feel utterly unworthy? How does it feel to bear the weight of an entire people's hopes and fears on your shoulders, knowing that your own fate is bound to something greater than yourself? *The Epic of Moses* dives into these questions with fierce emotional depth, capturing the human heart behind the biblical legend.

---

1. https://books2read.com/u/49Koep

2. https://books2read.com/u/49Koep

From the burning bush to the mighty Exodus, from the trials of the desert to the moment he gazes upon the Promised Land he will never enter, Moses' story unfolds with power and poetry. This is a man who was not born a hero but became one by answering a call beyond his own understanding. His life was marked by moments of divine wonder and searing pain, and through it all, his unwavering faith in the God who led him forward transformed him—and the course of history itself.

As you read, you will feel the pulse of a nation longing for freedom, the roar of a prophet speaking truth to power, and the inner conflict of a servant torn between his doubts and his destiny. Through vivid, lyrical language and rich imagery, this poem reveals the heart of Moses—his fears, his sacrifices, and his unyielding devotion to God's promise.

This is more than just a retelling of an ancient tale. It is a meditation on the very nature of leadership, faith, and purpose. It's about finding strength in the face of adversity and believing in something greater than yourself, even when the path is unclear. It's about the timeless journey of trusting that God's plan for you is bigger than your own limitations.

The Epic of Moses is a tribute to the power of God's call, the price of obedience, and the courage to stand firm in the face of impossible odds. Whether you are familiar with the biblical account or new to Moses' story, this powerful poem will pull you into a world of ancient wonders and timeless truths.

Take a step into Moses' world and be transformed. The journey awaits.
Read more at www.AlexTelman.com.